The **Muslim** Experience

J F Aylett and Kevin O'Donnell

rray

INE GROUP

seeking religion

Acknowledgements

The publishers would like to thank the following for permission to reproduce material in this book:

BBC Radio for the extract from *Quest*; BBC Television for the extract from *Third Eye*; Channel Four Television Company Ltd for the extracts from *Muslims in Britain*, a Priory Production for Channel 4 Television Company Ltd; Christian Education Movement for the extract from *RE Today*; The Muslim Educational Trust for the extracts from *The 4th Revised Edition of Islam Beliefs and Teachings* (1989); Time Life Books Inc for the extract from *Great Ages of Man: Early Islam* by Desmond Stewart and the Editors of Time Life Books, © 1967 Time Life Books Inc.; TVS Production Ltd for the extract from the *Human Factor* programme (1988); Unwin Hyman Ltd for the extract from *Rugs to Riches* by Caroline Bosley (1981).

Words in heavy type **like this** can be found in the glossary on page 63.

Orders: please contact Bookpoint Ltd, 130 Milton Park, Abingdon, Oxon OX14 SB. Telephone: (44) 01235 827720, Fax: (44) 01235 400454. Lines are open from 9.00–5.00, Monday to Saturday, with a 24 hour message answering service. You can also order through our website www.hoddereducation.co.uk

British Library Cataloguing in Publication Data
A catalogue record for this title is available from The British Library

ISBN-10: 0 340 74770 6
ISBN-13: 978 0 340 74770 4

First published 1991
Second edition 2000
Impression number   10   9
Year   2010   2009   2008   2007   2006

Cover photo from CIRCA Photo Library
All illustrations supplied by Daedalus, with special thanks to John McIntyre and Mohamed Abu Mustafa.
Typeset by Wearset, Boldon, Tyne and Wear.
Printed in Italy for Hodder Murray, an imprint of Hodder Education, a member of the Hodder Headline Group, 338 Euston Road, London NW1 3BH.

The authors and publishers thank the following for permission to reproduce copyright photographs in this book:

Associated Press AP: pp7r, 59; Mark Azavedo: p47; La Bibliotheque Nationale: p10; Circa Photo Library: pp4, 6t, 58r (William Holtby), 19l, 19br (Barrie Searle), 43, 55 (John Smith), 6b, 31, 54r; Corbis: p42; Edward Arnold: p12; Sonia Halliday Photographs: p16, 24l; Life File: p27l (Dave Thompson); Christine Osborne/MEP: pp11, 40 (Camerapix), 21, 23, 24r, 30, 33, 34, 35, 37, 39, 41, 44, 45, 46, 50, 51, 52, 53, 54l, 57, 58l, 60, 62; David Rose: pp7l, 8, 19tr, 27r, 32, 49; Jan Thompson: p17; Topkapi Museum: p22; Travel Ink: p48 (Joanna Wilsher).

Every effort has been made to contact the holders of copyright material but if any have been inadvertently overlooked, the publishers will be pleased to make the necessary alterations at the first opportunity.

Notes:
Whenever Muslims speak or write Muhammad's name, they usually add 'Peace be upon him'. (Sometimes written as 'pbuh'.) It is a sign of respect. This book does not do so, but this is not intended to be disrespectful. A Muslim who reads aloud from this book may wish to add these words wherever the Prophet's name occurs.

Dates in this book are given as:

CE = Common Era
BCE = Before the Common Era

CE corresponds to AD, and BCE corresponds to BC. The years are the same, but CE and BCE can be used by anyone, regardless of their religion. (AD and BC are Christian: AD stands for Anno Domini – in the Year of Our Lord, i.e. Jesus Christ; BC stands for Before Christ.)

Contents

◀ *These Muslim children live in Isfahan in Iran*

Muslims can be from any nation or race, anywhere in the world. Islam is an international faith. The religion is called 'Islam,' and a follower of it is a 'Muslim'.

You might notice that the two words contain the letters 'slm'. In Arabic, 'slm' forms words that mean either peace or submission. 'Islam' can be translated either as 'way of peace' or 'way of submission'. A Muslim, then, is 'one who finds peace' or 'one who submits'.

The idea is that a person finds peace in life by submitting to the will of God. This can be seen in the first sura (chapter) of the Muslim holy book, the Qur'an, which is recited when Muslims pray:

- In the name of Allah, the Compassionate, the Merciful, King of Judgement Day! You alone we worship, and to You alone we pray for help. *Guide us to the straight path*, the path of those whom You have favoured, not of those who have incurred Your wrath, nor of those who have gone astray.

Again, the Qur'an says:

- It was He who sent down tranquillity into the hearts of the faithful so that their faith might grow stronger.

(48:4)

We have many choices in life, and selfish actions can take us down the wrong path and cause a great deal of hurt, both to others and ourselves. A Muslim would add that we can offend God, too.

▲ *Which is the right path?*

We choose our own behaviour. Many times, in everyday life, we have to choose right or wrong paths.

Muslims believe that their faith helps them to see which is the right path, the straight path which leads to peace.

● What would you do?

John has been given a new CD player for his birthday. It has all the latest technology and was very expensive. He brings it to school and shows it off. Michael watches him and would really like one, just the same. But there is no way he can afford to buy one. Paula wants to buy some new clothes at the weekend. She decides to steal the CD player and sell it to Michael for whatever he can afford. She will be happy to get £20 for it.

Paula sees her chance when the class is doing PE. She slips into the teacher's office and takes the CD player, passing it out through the window to Rachel, who will get a cut of the money once it is sold. Rachel runs off and hides it in a plastic bag in the bushes at the edge of the school grounds. She is on a cross-country run, and so no one suspects.

When the lesson is over, John asks for his CD player back. There is panic when it cannot be found and everyone's belongings are searched. It is nowhere to be found. The headteacher and the school office are informed. John phones home and his father immediately phones the police, though the school do not know this.

Paula offers the CD player to Michael. He is sorely tempted. This is the only chance he is going to have to own such a piece of equipment.

5

▲ Paula, Michael and John making choices

> In groups, work out two role plays. In one, Michael buys the CD player. In the other, he thinks about it and refuses. Maybe he is called 'chicken' and other names in the process. Try to think what consequences would follow from Michael's actions. How would he feel?

1 A _____ follows the religion of _____.
2 What two things does 'Islam' mean?
3 Why are these two things like the two sides of the same coin?

4 Find a line in the passage of the Qur'an which suggests that following God will bring peace.

"As-Islām"

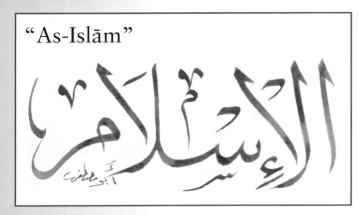

▲ *'Islam' written in Arabic*

Islam began in Arabia, and so Muslims learn Arabic and their Scriptures and prayers are written in Arabic letters. These can be highly decorative.

▲ *A prayer mat*

Muslims use prayer mats which they unroll and kneel upon as a mark of respect, so that they are praying upon clean ground. Many Muslims are recognised by this custom. Muslims face a holy building, the **Ka'bah**, in Makkah, which is in Arabia, when they pray.

▲ *Mosques can be recognised by their domes and minarets*

Muslim places of worship are called **mosques**. These can be in a converted house, or school hall, but specially built ones will have two distinctive features – a tower and a dome.

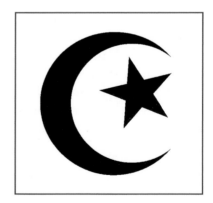

▲ *Crescent moon and star – symbol of Islam*

This is the symbol of the Muslim faith:

● the five-pointed star can represent the five pillars, or main beliefs of Islam;
● the moon and the star speak about God's creation;
● a new star rises as the moon fades. Muslims believe that their religion renewed God's message on Earth, as had been taught by many prophets over the ages. The last of these was Muhammad.

It is unfortunate that many people in the West have a negative, **stereotyped** view of Muslims. The news often shows images of **extremist** groups who bomb and use violence in the name of God. Most Muslims are not like this, and they seek a more gentle, peaceful way of life. If people in a Muslim country only ever saw pictures of Catholic and Protestant terrorist groups in Northern Ireland, they would have a strange view of the Christian religion. Every religion has its extremists.

▲ *A Western terrorist*

The story of Aladdin is a popular children's tale. It comes from a Muslim country, and Aladdin's name, in Arabic, means 'Servant of Allah'. 'Allah' is Arabic for 'the God', literally, 'the one God'.

▲ *A Muslim commits him or herself to God and prays for peace*

▲ *'Allah is the Greatest'*

1 Copy out the Arabic writing for 'Islam,' and for 'Allah'.
2 What does 'Allah' actually mean?
3 Why do Muslims learn Arabic?
4 Draw the symbol for the Muslim faith.
5 Design a symbol for something that means a great deal to you.
6 See if you can find out where the nearest mosque is to your school.

◀ *Breathtaking beauty*

Some things in life take your breath away. Think of watching a beautiful sunrise, with morning birdsong in your ears. A waterfall, the stillness deep inside a forest, or the staggering height of a mountain range can bring tears to your eyes, or send tingles down the spine. So can the arrival of a new baby.

Have you ever had an experience of overwhelming beauty?

The experience of the stunning beauty in nature, starting with a hike in the mountains of Oregon, was a turning point for one young woman:

- I felt a tremendous sense of joy and realised that if this beauty was in everything around me, in every scrap of matter, then it must also be within me. My heart broke open and my soul leapt free, exulting in this moment of inter-connection.

This opened her up to start believing in God. The existence of God cannot be proven; it is a matter of faith, but modern society likes to work with sure facts and experiments that prove x or y.

- The existence of God can only be felt in the soul; it cannot be measured with a ruler or proved with a calculation, therefore God does not exist. It is that simple.

Muslims believe that God is the creator of the universe, and all beauty and life comes from Allah as a gift.

In Muslim countries you are awakened by the early morning call to prayer, echoing from mosque to mosque: 'Come to prayer. Prayer is better than sleep. God is worthy of such praise.'

Muslims worship Allah out of gratitude for their lives and the world around them.

The One and Only

Most religions teach that there is only one God, one Big Answer behind all things. This has not always been the case, though. Many ancient tribes believed in many gods – one of the wind, one of the earth, one of fire, and so on. Gradually, through the message of teachers and prophets, many started to believe that there was one force that lay behind everything. This was simpler and **sublime**. The vast universe of many galaxies and forces is really all one thing – God's creation. God then demanded *all* our thanks and praise. We did not owe so much to this god, and so much to that one. Imagine what it would be like trying to love a number of girlfriends or boyfriends at once! We need to give our hearts to one.

"Ar-Raḥmān"	The Merciful	الرَّحْمٰن
"Al-Khāliq"	The Creator	الخَلِق
"Al-'Alīm"	The All-Knowing	العَلِيم
"Al-Wadūd"	The Loving	الوَدُود
"As-Salām"	The Source of Peace	السَّلام

▲ *Some of the beautiful names in Arabic*

Some Muslims recite these names in their prayers and meditations. They have prayer beads, with a name spoken on each bead passed through the fingers to count their praises.

Some of the beautiful names are written in English, below.

▲ *We can't love two people at once*

Muslims believe, very strongly, that there is one God – a mystery, a Spiritual Being that cannot and must not be pictured in human ways. 'Allah' is not his personal name, but a title, 'the one God'. The Qur'an reveals various titles for God, known as 'the ninety-nine beautiful names'.

▲ *The Qur'an contains ninety-nine names of God. These are some of them*

1 Talk about times when you have felt that you have been overwhelmed by beauty.
2 Try a stilling exercise where you imagine that you are walking in the forest. You stop in the centre and listen to the sounds. The odd branch snaps, a nut falls, a bird flies. Then listen to the silence. After the exercise, describe the scene and the different things you heard.
3 Why is it easier and simpler to worship one God only?
4 What do Muslims recite on their prayer beads?
5 Look at the selection of names for God in the above picture.
   a) Choose one that means most to you at the moment.
   b) Draw this in a decorative design.
   c) Say why this one stood out from the rest.
   d) Can you think of another 'beautiful name' for God from everyday, modern life?

A Man called Muhammad

About the year 570 CE a baby boy was born in Makkah (Mecca), in what is now Saudi Arabia. The boy was Muhammad.

His father had died weeks earlier. It was the custom in his tribe for new-born babies to be fed by a **foster-mother**. So at first Muhammad was looked after by a **Bedouin** woman.

When he was six, his mother died and he went to live with his grandfather. Just two years later, his grandfather also died and Muhammad was looked after by his uncle, a merchant.

A legend says that a Christian monk met the boy and was impressed by him. He said that this young man would be a **prophet** in the future.

As a boy, Muhammad looked after sheep in the desert. When he grew up, he was proud of this work. 'Allah,' he told people, 'sent no prophet who was not a shepherd.'

Muhammad went on to become a camel driver and, later, a trader. He was honest and a hard worker and was spotted by a rich widow called Khadijah. She was a trader and asked him to look after her business affairs.

He was a good businessman. On his first trip to Syria, he earned Khadijah nearly twice the money that she expected. Soon afterwards, she asked Muhammad to marry her.

Muhammad's uncle advised the young man to accept. So, aged twenty-five, Muhammad married Khadijah, who was older than him. It was a happy marriage. They had six children, two boys and four girls.

▶ This old picture shows a Muslim merchant setting off on a journey

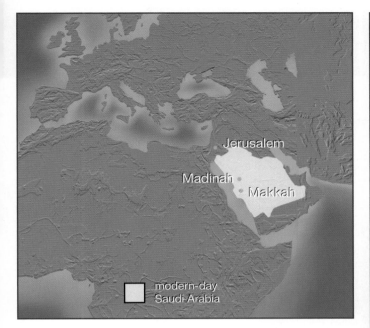

▲ *Saudi Arabia*

▲ *The Ka'bah in Makkah. This is where Muslims face when they pray*

Makkah was already a religious city. **Pilgrims** flocked to see the black stone which was kept in the Ka'bah. The tribes thought that this had come from heaven – a gift from the gods. One year, heavy rain damaged the walls of the Ka'bah; repairs were needed. Four tribes would share the work.

All went well until the time came to put the black stone in place. Then the arguments began. Which tribe should have the honour of doing it? The quarrels were so bitter that it even looked as though a **civil war** might break out.

In the end, an old man had an idea. They would let the gods help. The first person to walk through the temple gates next day would be asked to sort it out. The first person turned out to be Muhammad.

People already called him 'the honest one', so he seemed a good person to solve the dispute. His solution was very clever. He took a cloak and spread it on the ground. The black stone was placed on top and leaders from each tribe took hold of the corners of the cloak. Holding tight, they lifted the stone into place. Then, Muhammad slid it into position.

Muslims do not draw pictures of Muhammad. They believe it is wrong. But their holy books give this description of him:
Handsome; medium height; thick black hair and beard; wide forehead; heavy eyebrows; large dark eyes below long lashes; wide chest and shoulders.

1 Copy out and complete this paragraph:
  Muhammad's mother died when he was _____ and he was later looked after by an _____ . He worked as a _____ and later with camels. Aged 25, he married _____ and they had _____ children.

2 **a)** Write down any words from this list which you think describe a good shepherd: reliable; kind; quick-tempered; watchful; calm; lazy; caring; understanding; thin; patient; loving.
  b) Which of these qualities are also useful for dealing with people? Give a reason for each answer.

3 **a)** Read the story about the black stone. Why was Muhammad's solution clever?
  b) Why do you think people did not resent him sliding the stone into place?
  c) Can you think of a time in your life when someone has solved a problem in a clever way?
  d) Write your own story about a problem that no one can solve until a stranger comes along with a bright idea.

◀ *The cave on Mount Nur where Muslims believe Muhammad lived during the month of Ramadan*

From then onwards, Muhammad spent more time **meditating**. He was upset by the way the people of Makkah lived their lives. He wanted to be alone to think. Each year, during the month of Ramadan, he went alone to a cave called Hira on Mount Nur, outside the city. He did this until he was forty years old. That year was his fifth at the cave – and he had a surprise visitor.

One night, an angel appeared to Muhammad. 'Read,' he told Muhammad. But Muhammad could not read or write. Three times, Muhammad told the angel that he was not a reader; three times, the angel squeezed him hard. Then, the angel taught Muhammad this verse:

> ● Read in the name of your Lord who created.
> Created man from a **clot** of blood.
> Read, your Lord is most Generous.
> Who taught by the pen.
> Taught man what he did not know.
>
> Qur'an 96:1–5

One of his wife's Christian relations told Muhammad he had seen God's messenger, the angel Gabriel. At first, Muhammad had been frightened. But his wife reassured him. She told him it was a sign that he had been chosen as a prophet.

Months later, he had another **vision** of the angel Gabriel. This really frightened Muhammad and he rushed home. Once again, his wife comforted him. This time, Muhammad made up his mind. God *had* chosen him as a prophet.

> ● O Khadijah, the time of slumber and rest is past. Gabriel has asked me to warn men and call them to Allah and to His worship. But whom shall I call? And who will listen to me?

So Muhammad began to preach that there was one God. The first people who listened were his wife and a young cousin. However, Muhammad's message slowly spread among the people in Makkah. Few people took it seriously.

The people of Makkah did not live good lives. Many of the men fought and were cruel to the women and children. They drank a lot. Above all, they worshipped **idols** – great stone statues in the city. The Ka'bah was used to house some of these idols; people danced round the Ka'bah to worship them.

Muhammad told them not to pray to these idols. His message was simple. There is only one God and he created the world. It was wicked to worship statues.

◄ Yathrib was later called Madinah-al-Nabi – the City of the Prophet. Today, it is still called Madinah (Medina). This green dome is built there above Muhammad's tomb

The merchants of Makkah were angry. Pilgrims came to visit their **pagan shrines**. It brought business into the city. They did not want Muhammad wrecking it. So they said he was a liar or a madman. Some of his followers were beaten up or tortured – and the attacks grew worse.

One day, pilgrims from the city of Yathrib heard Muhammad preach and were impressed. They invited him to go and live with them, over 300 km away across the Arabian desert. Muhammad accepted their invitation.

This is an important event for Muslims. They call it the hijrah, which means departure. Even today, the Muslim system of dating years starts with Muhammad's journey, so the Islamic calendar begins in 622 CE (1AH). (AH means After Hijrah.)

In Madinah, Muhammad started the first Muslim community. The first mosque was built there and Muhammad's house was next door. Muhammad himself even helped to build the mosque. He taught that everyone was equal in the eyes of God. He mended his own clothes and did his own shopping. He wanted to be a good example to his people.

● A woman came with a garment which she had made especially for the Prophet. He gracefully accepted it and wore it. Coming to an **assembly** he was met by a man who touched it and said, 'Give it to me, O Messenger of God'. The Prophet said, 'With pleasure!' Having stayed for some time at the meeting, he went home, took off the garment, wrapped it up and sent it to the man who had asked for it, [although] he was in sore need of it himself.

1 Write one sentence about each of these words: prophet; vision; idol; pagan; shrine; hijrah.

2 Write about a time when you had to get away from some trouble. Is it always cowardly to do this, or is it sometimes wise?

3 a) Work in pairs. One of you is from Yathrib and the other is one of Muhammad's followers. The person from Yathrib is trying to persuade the Muslim to come to Yathrib. Write down your conversation.

4 a) Still in pairs, write an **obituary** notice for Muhammad. One of you should write what a Muslim might have written. The other should write what a merchant from Makkah might have written.

b) Now, compare your obituaries. What differences are there – and why?

▲ *Each of us is unique, one of a kind*

Each person is special, one of a kind. The way our bodies work is amazing – our eyes can see more than the largest telescope we can make; our lungs, if disentangled and spread out, are large enough to cover a tennis court; we send a message to our brain at 124 mph when we touch something; and our eyes can distinguish up to one million surface colours.

All the muscle, tissue, chemicals and charges form a living being that is capable of thought and feeling. We each have our own personality. No matter how much we might be like other members of our families, we are still different.

Muhammad wanted the Arabs to remember who their Creator was. Each human life is unique, original and sacred. Life is given as a gift. As the angel had said to him:

> ● 'Read in the name of the Lord who created.
>   Created man from a clot of blood . . .'

If we treat each other as special and as God's sacred creations, then the world would be a more peaceful place. The Qur'an says, 'Whoever killed a human being . . . should be looked upon as though he had killed all mankind; and that whoever saved a human life should be regarded as though he had saved all mankind.' (5:32)

1 Design a poster about yourself saying 'I'm Unique!' Include hobbies, photos, favourite things and music.
2 Think of the greatest gift that you have ever been given.
3 Write a short story where a king sends his servants to find out what the greatest gift ever given to anyone has been. One returns to reveal that it is the gift of life.

Islam Spreads

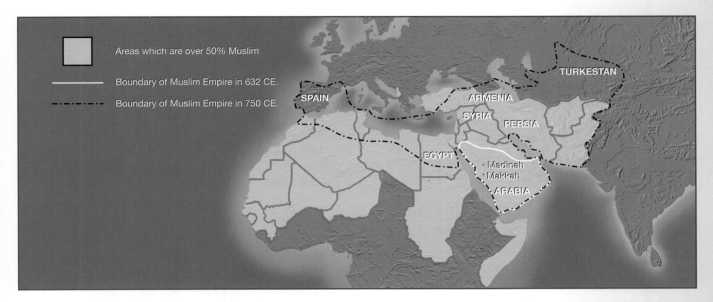

Areas which are over 50% Muslim

Boundary of Muslim Empire in 632 CE.

Boundary of Muslim Empire in 750 CE.

SPAIN ARMENIA TURKESTAN SYRIA PERSIA EGYPT Madinah Makkah ARABIA

▲ *How the Muslim Empire grew in the hundred years after Muhammad's death. The key shows how Islam is still the main religion in these areas today*

When Muhammad first arrived in Madinah, he hoped that the local Jews would become Muslims. Muhammad himself followed some Jewish religious practices. However, the Jews felt threatened by the new religion. So Muhammad concentrated on gaining support among the Arabs.

In 630 CE, Muhammad himself led 10,000 men in a march to Makkah because the Makkans had broken a **treaty**. The Makkans put up little resistance. Muhammad entered the Ka'bah and destroyed the pagan idols. From now onwards it would be a Muslim shrine. He also sent out letters to other rulers, asking them to become Muslims.

However, the real spread of Islam did not begin until after Muhammad's death. Then, his good friend Abu Bakr was chosen to be Caliph. It means *successor*. He told the people:

- I have been chosen by you as your leader, although I am no better than any one of you. If I do any good, give me your support. If I do any wrong, set me right ... Obey me as long as I obey Allah and His messenger. If I disobey Allah and His messenger, you are free to disobey me.

Under his leadership, the tribes of Arabia were united in following Islam. Their new religion stopped them from fighting each other. But further north, the great **empires** of Byzantium and Persia had long been enemies.

These empires taxed neighbouring Arabs to pay for their own wars. Naturally, the Arabs resented this. When the Muslims began to move north, the Arabs saw a chance to gain their freedom. Many joined the Muslims in fighting their former masters.

Within a hundred years of Muhammad's death, Muslims had built up an empire which included north Africa to the south. In the east, they had crossed India and reached China; to the west, they had entered southern France.

It was natural that Muslims should also want to spread their religion. However, the Qur'an clearly says that 'There is no **compulsion** in religion'. So Christians and Jews in the empire were allowed to keep their own religions. Both Jews and Christians often preferred to be ruled by Muslims than by pagans.

The Qur'an teaches that Muslims should not fight unless it is in self defence.

'To those on whom war is made, permission is given to fight ...'
(22:39)

Aggress not: God loves not the aggressors.' (2:187)

The early Muslim armies fought back when neighbouring rulers tried to stop people worshipping as Muslims. They defended their rights and their lands and this led to the birth of a great Muslim Empire.

The great Arab Muslim empire was destroyed in the thirteenth century. But Islam itself went on spreading. In Africa, Muslim traders carried Muhammad's message south far beyond the Muslim empire.

Trade also took Islam across the Indian Ocean. Muslim merchants had for years been spreading their beliefs east in Malaysia and Indonesia. A chain of towns was set up down the east coast of Africa five hundred years before Portuguese explorers arrived – and destroyed them.

The Arab commander Khalid besieged Damascus. When the people gave in, he told them this:

- In the name of Allah, the **compassionate**, the merciful, this is what Khalid ibn al-Walid would grant to the people of Damascus ... He promises to give them security for their lives, property and churches. Their city wall shall not be demolished. No Muslim shall be quartered in their houses. We give to them the pact of Allah and the protection of His Prophet ... So long as they pay the tax, nothing but good shall befall them.

▶ *These Muslim travellers are being welcomed as they pass through a Syrian town in the thirteenth century*

1 Match up the words on the left with the correct meanings from the right.

Ka'bah	Muslims' holy book
Qur'an	the religion of Muslims
Abu Bakr	cube-shaped building in Makkah
Islam	Muhammad's successor

2 a) Look at the map on page 15. Using an atlas, write down the names of at least eight modern countries which were part of the Muslim empire in 750 CE.

b) Write down any of these eight countries which are not mainly Muslim today.

3 a) Why do you think Muslims wanted to spread their religion?

b) Why didn't they force Christians or Jews to become Muslims?

c) Read what Khalid said to the people of Damascus. Do you think he was being fair? Give reasons.

4 Is it right to force anyone to act against their conscience or beliefs? Can you think of a time when this has happened to you?

Muslims honour Jesus Christ as a great prophet. They believe that God has always sent prophets to humankind, from Adam onwards. Muslims believe in the same prophets as Jews and Christians, and the names of Noah, Abraham, Moses and others can be found in the Qur'an. Muhammad is seen as the Last Prophet, or 'the Seal of the Prophets', whose message has been faithfully preserved in the text of the Qur'an. He closes the line of prophets, as a wax seal used to seal and close a letter.

Qur'anic name	Biblical name
Adam	Adam
Idrīs	Enoch
Nūh	Noah
Hūd	
Sālih	
Ibrāhīm	Abraham
Ismā'īl	Ishmael
Ishaq	Isaac
Lūt	Lot
Ya'qūb	Jacob
Yūsuf	Joseph
Shu'ayb	
Ayyūb	Job
Mūsa	Moses
Hārūn	Aaron
Dhu'l-kifl	Ezekiel
Daūd	David
Sulaymān	Solomon
Iliās	Elias/Elijah
Al-Yasa'	Elisha
Yunūs	Jonah
Zakariyya	Zechariah
Yahya	John
'Isa	Jesus
Muhammad	

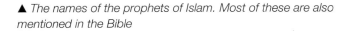

▲ *The names of the prophets of Islam. Most of these are also mentioned in the Bible*

In Arabic, in the Qur'an, Jesus is called Isa ibn Mariam al Masih – 'Jesus, son of Mary, the Messiah'.

▲ *A Christian picture of Jesus Christ. Jesus was the prophet before Muhammad, according to Muslims*

Jesus was the prophet before Muhammad, and a special reverence is given to him. Muslims believe that he was a perfect human being who was born from a virgin. Allah performed a miracle in Mary's womb as a sign that this boy was to be a special prophet. The Qur'an teaches that Jesus worked miracles, healing people. He is also called 'Messiah', 'God's specially chosen and anointed'.

In the Qur'an, Jesus says, 'I am the servant of Allah. He has given me the Gospel and ordained me a prophet. His blessing is upon me wherever I go, and He has commanded me to be steadfast in prayer and to give alms to the poor as long as I shall live.' (19:29)

Muslims do not believe that Jesus was divine – Christians say that he was God living in a man (this belief is known as 'the incarnation'). Muhammad once said, 'Do not extol me as the Christians have extolled the Son of Mary. I am only God's servant. Refer to me as the servant and messenger of God.'

Most Muslims believe that Jesus was too holy to die on the cross: they believe another died in his place, or a trick was played upon the crowd, and he was taken up to heaven to be with God. Muslims expect Jesus to return before the Final Judgement. Muhammad once said, 'I swear by Him who holds my life between His hands, the son of Mary will come back down among you very soon as a just judge.'

The sections of the Qur'an which speak of the fate of Jesus are slightly **obscure**, and some scholars feel that the Arabic can be understood differently. A **minority** opinion is that Jesus might have been crucified, but could not be spiritually killed, and he was taken to heaven.

Muhammad once spoke of a vision of Jesus he had had:

> ● 'Then I noticed a brown-skinned man with smooth hair which was wet; water was dripping from it onto the ground between his legs. I asked who it was and was told, "It's the son of Mary" ...'

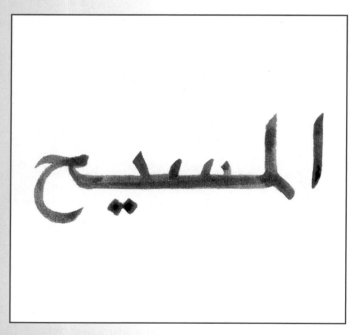

▲ al-Masih, The Messiah, written in Arabic

Whatever exactly happened to Jesus, all Muslims believe that he was taken to be with God and will one day return.

Christians call Jesus 'the Son of God'. Muslims disagree for the Qur'an teaches that Allah has no son. The Qur'an does say that Jesus was specially blessed by Allah, born of a virgin, a worker of miracles, and he is even described as 'a word sent from Allah'.

The Christian term 'Son of God' is often misunderstood – it is not meant in a physical sense. It is more poetic, meaning that Jesus was the most holy person who ever lived, filled with God. (Christians also call Jesus 'the Word of God'.) There are still major disagreements between Muslims and Christians about Jesus, but many try to respect each other's beliefs as they share and talk together.

---

1 List all the titles that Jesus is given in the Qur'an. What do these things suggest about him?

2 Why is Muhammad called 'the seal of the prophets'?

3 What do most Muslims believe happened to Jesus?

4 How is Jesus described in Muhammad's vision? Why is this likely to be how Jesus would have looked?

5 a) What do Christians believe about Jesus as 'Son of God'?

b) What does the Qur'an say about God having a son?

▲ *The Western Wall*

▲ *The Dome of the Rock*

▲ *The Church of the Holy Sepulchre*

Jerusalem is a city holy to three faiths – Jews, Christians and Muslims. The photographs above show the Western Wall – sacred to the Jews; the Dome of the Rock – a sacred mosque for Muslims; and the Church of the Holy Sepulchre – a sacred site for Christians.

At first, Muhammad and the Muslims faced Jerusalem when they prayed, as this was the holy city of the Jews and the Christians. This was changed to Makkah after the Muslims were **opposed** by local Jews. Makkah, after all, contained the Ka'bah which was said to have been built upon a sacred site. Here, Abraham had nearly sacrificed his son and earlier, Adam, the first man, was said to have built a temple to worship God.

Muhammad had an experience where he was taken by angels to Jerusalem, to the mountain upon which the Dome of the Rock mosque stands, and he ascended into heaven to meet the prophets and to talk with Allah.

Sadly, the three faiths have fought each other over who controls the city of Jerusalem, and the territory around it. Much blood has been shed. There are still disputes today about who owns the land in this area.

The Crusades in the Middle Ages were the most bloodthirsty encounter between Christians and Muslims. Three Crusades were launched in the Holy Land as attempts to take back control of the holy places from the Muslims. (The Christian Crusaders wore the cross on their tunics as a sign of their faith in Christ. This was originally a badge for unarmed pilgrims, but soldiers later wore it.) There are still tensions in the Middle East between Muslims, Christians and Jews. Some of this trouble can be traced back to the hatred and mistrust unleashed during the Crusades.

For most of the time, the Muslims controlling the holy places were fair to Jews and Christians. When Jerusalem first fell to the Muslim Caliph Omar in 638 CE, the Patriarch Sophronius, the leader of the Christian Church there, escorted him into the city. The Patriarch took Omar into the Church of the Holy Sepulchre. Muslim teaching said that the holy places of the Christians and the Jews should be respected. He looked around, and then realised that it was time for the mid-day prayers. He carried his rolled-up prayer mat with him, and asked if there were somewhere that he could spread this out and pray. The Patriarch offered to let him pray within the shrine, but Omar refused. He was concerned that his more extreme followers would immediately claim the place for Islam. He left and prayed outside in the porch area. True to his words, this area was claimed for the Muslim faith afterwards. The Church itself was spared and was left in the hands of the Christians, who could worship there and come and go on pilgrimage freely.

How different was the story when the first Crusaders took control of Jerusalem again in 1099. The fanatical Crusaders slew all the Muslims and Jews that they could find. This massacre horrified the Muslim world, and many Christians in Europe, too.

The most famous Crusader to conquer Jerusalem was Richard the Lionheart of England (King Richard I). The Muslim leader at the time was Saladin, and the two men developed a great respect for each other. Saladin even sent a box of snow and fresh fruit to the king when he was ill with a fever.

Saladin is described as sincere and merciful – he set many prisoners free, and was moved to tears when a Christian woman begged him to find her daughter. She had been captured and taken as a slave. With a word from Saladin, a man was sent out to search for her. She was soon found and reunited with her mother.

Richard could be unspeakably cruel, however. When he captured the coastal town of Acre, he had thousands of Muslim men executed. He was afraid that if they went free they would rejoin Saladin and fight against him. Christian crusaders killed in the name of God and some of them were far from holy.

Sadly, these vicious actions have led to centuries of mistrust between Christians and Muslims. At the end of the twentieth century, Pope John Paul II, leader of the Roman Catholic Church, apologised for the Crusades as a terrible error that the Church had made all those years ago, and other Christians took part in a Walk of Reconciliation to all the places visited by the Crusaders, to pray and ask forgiveness for the hatred that had gone on in the past.

▲ This drawing shows Richard jousting with Saladin, whose helmet comes off to reveal his devilish features. Who was more bloodthirsty, though – Richard or Saladin?

1 a) Match up the holy place to the right faith:

Christian   The Western Wall

Muslim   The Church of the Holy Sepulchre

Jewish   The Dome of the Rock

b) Find out why each place is special to each faith.

2 a) Look at the drawing of Richard fighting with Saladin. From the information on this page, say who you think should have worn the devil's face, and give reasons.

b) Imagine that you are the Christian woman begging Saladin to rescue your daughter. Write down what you would say to him.

c) What have the Pope and some other Christians done at the end of the twentieth century to try to make up for all the killing in the Crusades?

3 a) Do you think two people with different views can get along as friends?

b) Write a short story about a conflict between two people or groups.

c) In real life, can you think of a time when you have needed to say sorry?

▲ *These Muslims will pray quietly before their journey begins*

Before Muslims eat their food, or go on a journey, they will say a quiet prayer to themselves:

'Bismillah ir-rahman ir-rahim.'

This means 'In the name of Allah the Compassionate, the Merciful.'

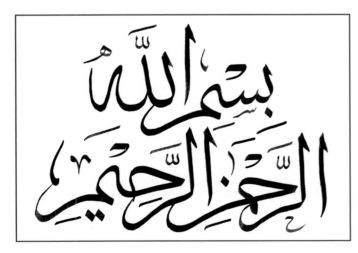

▲ *The bismillah prayer in Arabic*

The phrase 'bismillah' might only be familiar to many Westerners from the pop song 'Bohemian Rhapsody' by Queen, but in this it is used as a throw-away line. To a Muslim, bismillah is a sacred phrase, summing up so much about God. 'God is Compassionate and Merciful.' The Arabic words for these two attributes both come from the word for 'womb' and suggest life-giving care.

Muslims are forbidden to picture God in any shape or form – God is mysterious and beyond us. A Christian girl once said that as a child she imagined God to be a loving presence that enveloped the world like a big womb, like a holy mother. This suggests the same ideas of life-giving care that the 'bismillah' states.

Muslims pray certain prayers in Arabic for their faith began in Arabia. Their holy book, the Qur'an, was written in Arabic. 'Qur'an' means **'Recitation'**. This comes from the angel's command in Muhammad's first vision, 'Read in the name of your Lord who created you . . .'

Muslims believe the Qur'an is the word of God, exactly as the Angel Gabriel revealed it to Muhammad. It was not revealed all at once to Muhammad, but in parts over twenty-three years.

As Muhammad could not write, he chose people to write it down. Few other Arabs could read in those days either but they did have a gift for learning long stories and poems by heart.

Today, all Muslims learn parts of the Qur'an by heart. Some people can recite it all. Such a person is called a hafiz. The Qur'an contains about 78 000 words. (This book has around 21 500.)

After Muhammad's death, many Muslims were killed in battle. Abu Bakr was worried that the Qur'an might be lost, so he ordered a standard copy to be made. This was checked by those who had heard it direct from Muhammad himself. This copy was made less than two years after Muhammad died. All modern copies are the same as this.

The book was revealed to Muhammad in Arabic, a language which most Muslims can still read. Muslims do not believe it is possible to translate it perfectly. In any case, they believe it is a beautiful book and the beauty becomes lost in any other language.

A true Muslim reads the Qur'an every day. It gives guidance for everyone on how to live a good life. It explains how to serve God. Muslims believe it is the final word of God to human beings, and that it is therefore perfect.

Although the Qur'an is the Muslims' holy book, they also consult books called the Hadith. These are collections of the words and actions of Muhammad himself. If Muslims face a problem, they may well read the Hadith to see if Muhammad ever coped with a similar problem. Then, they could follow his advice.

▶ There are two original copies of the Qur'an in the world today. This one is kept in Istanbul. The Qur'an is divided into 114 chapters, called suras. The first ones are the longest

Because they believe that the Qur'an contains the actual words of God, Muslims treat it with great respect. Before reading it, they first wash themselves. Copies of the Qur'an are kept wrapped up and are often put on a shelf to keep them safe.

Muslims believe that the Qur'an is God's message. That message tells them that there is only one God who created the world and everything in it. In the Qur'an, he provides his followers with a complete set of rules for daily life. This is how one Muslim teenager describes it.

> ● It tells us what the right things are and what the wrong things are. It tells us what to do and what not to do. So that way we keep the straight path. We've got the Qur'an to guide us and we've got the prophet Muhammad's sayings. So it helps us.

We asked some Muslims for their favourite part of the Qur'an. This is what a young woman said:

> ● I read **Sura Yasin** every day. People say it helps to make the day go by very easily. It is called 'the heart of the Qur'an'. The Prophet encouraged Muslims to read this chapter regularly.

This is what an **imam** said:

> ● Some chapters are favourite to me because they're very telling. For instance, we have a chapter called the Quraish. It refers to the tribe where the Prophet actually was born and he mentioned two major blessings – free from hunger and free from fear. I find this situation really the most important in people's lives.

▲ These copies of the Qur'an have been wrapped in cloth and placed on a shelf to protect them

1 Answer these questions in complete sentences:
  a) What is the holy book of Islam called?
  b) In what language is it written?
  c) Why do Muslims believe it is holy?
  d) Why do you think Muslims read it every day?

2 **a)** How do Muslims show their respect for the Qur'an? (You should find at least three answers.)
  b) How else could they show their respect?

3 **a)** Read the quotation from the Qur'an. What do you think the 'straight path' is?
  b) How did the Imam pick his favourite passage from the Qur'an?

  c) Does this mean that he and the young woman read the Qur'an for different reasons? Explain your answer.

4 **a)** Can you think of some good advice that someone close to you has given you? How did this help you?
  b) Try to remember what was said and write this down, decoratively, on a sheet of paper. Tie this up with ribbon and keep it somewhere private. Read this from time to time to remind yourself.
  c) Think of three rules for living that you think everyone should follow. Write these out on a page of your exercise book. Decorate this with a hand-drawn illustration or a picture from a magazine.

Muslims are expected to believe – *and act on their beliefs.* It is not enough just to believe or just to act. A Muslim's actions are based on the following beliefs.

One God (Allah)

Islam teaches that there is only one God. He has no family or partners. He is the only one whom people should worship. Every day, a Muslim says several times: 'There is no god but Allah and Muhammad is His Messenger.' This is known as the Shahadah – the confession of faith. If someone converts to Islam, they then have to say the Shahadah in front of Muslim witnesses.

> O my dear son! Do not make any partner to Allah. Truly, making anyone partner to Allah is a big **sin**.
>
> Qur'an 31:13

His Angels

Islam teaches that angels are God's servants who carry out his orders. They brought God's message to the prophets, including Muhammad himself. Other angels spend their time keeping records of human actions. But they cannot be seen by us.

His Books

Muslims believe that God has given all humans guidance through his prophets. There have been a number of holy books, including the original versions of the Law of Moses, the Psalms of David and the Gospel of Jesus. But only the Qur'an has not been changed by human beings. So only the Qur'an is perfect and will never change. The Qur'an is therefore the final word of God.

His Prophets

The Qur'an mentions twenty-five prophets by name. Most of them also appear in the Bible. The first was Adam and the last was Muhammad. Muslims believe they were all sent by God to show people how He wanted them to live.

The Day of Judgment

When this day comes, Muslims believe that all dead people will come to life and be questioned about their lives. It will not be the effect of their actions that matters; it will be what people *intended* their actions should do.

When this happens, God will judge us. Only God can judge and only God can forgive the wicked. People earn this forgiveness through prayers and actions.

> Actions shall be judged only by intention. A man shall get what he intends.
>
> Sahih Al-Bukhari (Hadith)

▲ *Young Muslims praying in London*

ISLAM

1
SHAHADAH
DECLARATION OF FAITH

2

3

4

5

لا إله إلا الله محمد رسول الله

There is no god but Allah and Muhammad is His Messenger

▲ *Islam is like a house supported by five pillars. The first of these is the declaration of faith: 'There is no god but Allah and Muhammad is His Messenger'*

The Will of God

Muslims believe that God has created the world and, at all times, remains in control of the world. He has complete knowledge of what will happen in the world. However, people face many choices each day. They can do bad or they can do good. God expects people to make choices. So we are still responsible for our actions.

Life After Death

Islam teaches that those who obey God will go to Paradise. There, they will live forever a life of peace and happiness. Many who disobey God will go to Hell, where life will be miserable. No one can say how God will judge anyone – some wrongdoers will be forgiven. Only God knows exactly what it is like in Paradise and Hell. Muhammad said there were things in Paradise which no eye has ever seen, no ear ever heard and no one can imagine.

● If anyone has got an **atom** of pride in his heart, he will not enter Paradise.

Sahih Al-Bukhari

1 Draw the diagram above. (You may miss out the Arabic writing, if you wish.) In later chapters, you will read about the other four pillars and can fill in the details.

2 **a)** Look at the painting of the angel. How is it shown?
b) What colours and things does the artist use to suggest that this is a holy, mysterious being?
c) If angels cannot be seen, why show them at all? This was taken from an old Muslim manuscript. Today, most Muslims would not even show an angel, for fear that people might worship it instead of Allah. They believe that spiritual beings are invisible, and beyond our imagination.

3 **a)** Think of an occasion when you did something you thought was wrong. Briefly, describe what you did.
b) What made you think it was wrong?
c) If you thought it was wrong, why did you do it?
d) Now, describe a time when you tried to do something good, but it went wrong.
e) Which of your two actions would a Muslim think was wrong? Explain how you decided.
f) Think back over the last week. Divide your page into two columns. Put a heading, MY BALANCE SHEET. In the left column, write down the good things you have done. On the right, write down the bad things.
g) What have you had to do to make up for some of the wrong things? How have they made you feel?

Beginning to Explore the Five Pillars

1 BELIEF

Letter	Arabic Pronunciation	Symbol
ا	alif	'
ب	ba'	b
ت	ta'	t
ث	tha'	s or t
ج	jīm	g or z
ح	Ha	H
خ	kha	kh
د	dal	d
ذ	thal	d or z
ر	ra	r
ز	za	z
س	sīn	s
ش	shīn	sh
ص	sād	*s*
ض	dād	*d*
ط	tā	*t*
ظ	thā	*z*
ع	ayn	"
غ	ghayn	gh
ف	fa'	f
ق	qāf	q or '
ك	kaf	k
ل	lam	l
م	mīm	m
ن	nūn	n
ه	ha	h
و	waw	w
ي	ya	yt

▲ *The Arabic alphabet*

The Shahadah in Arabic goes as follows:

'La illaha illal lahu. Muhammad rasulul la.'
'There is no god but Allah, and Muhammad is His Messenger.'

Using the Arabic alphabet, try to write this out in Arabic script. Remember that Arabic is written from right to left. The first word has been done for you.

"Lā"

▲ *'La', the first word of the Shahadah*

2 PRAYER

SAUDI ARABIA

• Makkah

▲ *Pointing the way to Makkah*

Using an atlas, find out how many degrees Makkah is from the UK. Then, using a compass, work out the direction of Makkah from the classroom. Design a sign that points the way to Makkah and display this in the right position. When Muslims say their formal daily prayers, they have to face the Ka'bah in Makkah.

3 GIVING MONEY

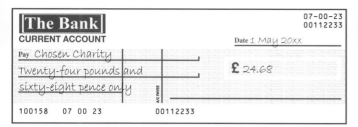

▲ *Giving to charity*

In groups, work out how much you all earn in a month from pocket money, odd jobs, paper rounds, and so on. Add it all up, and then work out what 2.5% of the total is. Decide upon a charity that this should go to (this is only make believe!). Draw the cheque and make it out to the charity for the correct amount.

A Muslim is expected to donate 2.5% of his or her savings each year. This is a compulsory payment. Muslims are encouraged to give to charity over and above this.

4 FASTING

▲ *Muslims sit in cafés but do not eat or drink during Ramadan*

Write out a list of all the things you drank and ate from breakfast until supper time yesterday. Then imagine a situation when the government banned people from eating and drinking in daylight hours. What would you do to stay alive?

Muslims are expected to fast in this way for the month of Ramadan. Yet, they do eat and drink at other times to stay alive. When do you think they will have to do this?

> These activities have been brief and simple introductions to the themes of the five pillars. The following chapters will explore these further.

5 PILGRIMAGE

▲ *Each of these young people will have made plans to spend a day at the concert*

Imagine that you wanted to go to a pop festival such as Glastonbury for the weekend with a group of friends. Make a list of all the things you would have to organise and plan for – transport, cost, food, buying tickets, where you were going to stay and what to take with you. If you think that being there is so important you will save up, plan ahead and go out of your way to do it.

Muslims try their best to visit Makkah at least once in their lifetime. This is a sacred place, a holy thing they are doing, and far more valuable than any mere music festival!

Discuss how much more they will plan, save and put themselves out to find spiritual blessing.

Muslims believe that God has created human beings to worship him. So the second pillar of Islam is prayer. Muslims must pray five times a day. Each time takes about ten minutes.

These five **compulsory** prayers are known as *salah*. They help Muslims to remember God and keep them from doing bad deeds. Muslims must still pray if they are ill or even fighting a war.

These five daily prayers do not mean that a Muslim cannot pray at other times. Other prayers, called *Du'a*, may be made at any time, anywhere. But all Muslims are expected to say salah. Once a week, on Fridays, there are special prayers called salah at mid-day instead of the normal mid-day prayers.

Men are asked to pray at mosques. However, if that is not possible, they may pray anywhere that is clean. Women are encouraged to pray at home. Every Muslim over the age of ten is generally made to perform these prayers. Children are taught to pray from any age, and custom varies.

All Muslims, wherever they are, face the Ka'bah when they perform salah. There is a special place in the mosque wall which shows them which way to face. Outside a mosque, some Muslims use a prayer mat with a compass in it.

This means that British Muslims face south-east when they pray. In Mexico, Muslims face east. In most of Africa, they face north-east.

- There's quite a lot of Muslim boys in our school. We have a separate room to pray in. Our headmaster is not **prejudiced**. One of the mothers asked him for a prayer room so they provided us with a special room. We only need to go there once for the afternoon prayer.

  Darwa

- There's nowhere in my school where I can go. So, at the end of the day, I just put my prayers together.

  Ali

1 Copy out this paragraph and fill in the gaps.
   Muslims must pray ____ times a day. This is called _____ . When they do this, they face the _____ . Other prayers are called _____ . These can be offered at any time.

2 **a)** Draw the diagram on this page.
   b) Which prayer do you think is most inconvenient? Give reasons for your choice.
   c) Why does Darwa only need the prayer room for the early afternoon prayers?

3 **a)** Look at the picture strip on page 29. Why do you think Muslims must wash themselves before praying?
   b) The following actions are all part of salah. Write them down in the order in which they are done.
   (i)   Stand and face Makkah
   (ii) Bow down with hands on knees
   (iii) Sit with knees bent
   (iv) Raise hands to ears
   (v)   The call to prayer

4 In groups, write down reasons why a Muslim might want to say Du'a. For instance, he or she might want to pray when a friend is ill. Afterwards, compare your answers.

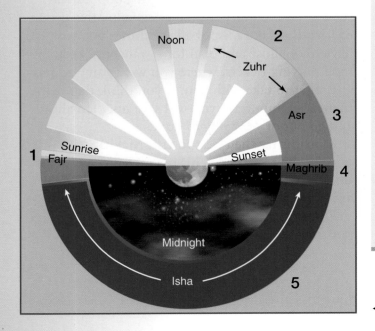

◀ *The times of daily prayer*

A Muslim must be clean. First, he performs Wudu (ablution).

He says

> In the name of Allah the most merciful, the most kind.

Both hands are washed up to the wrist.

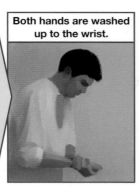

The mouth is rinsed three times.

The nostrils and tip of the nose are washed three times.

The face is washed three times, from right to left and from forehead to throat.

Each arm is washed three times.

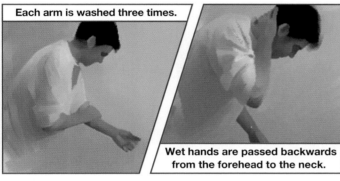

Wet hands are passed backwards from the forehead to the neck.

The ears and behind the ears are cleaned.

The nape is cleaned.

The feet are washed up to the ankles.

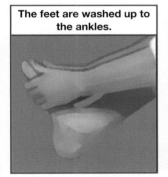

The Muslim says,

> I bear witness that there is no God but Allah and I bear witness that Muhammad is his servant and messenger.

THE CALL TO PRAYER

After the call to prayer, everyone faces the Ka'bah in Makkah.

Each Muslim says how many prayers he intends to say.

Women's positions are slightly different.

> Allahu Akbar.

(Allah is the greatest)

He recites the opening chapter of the Qur'an and any one other chapter.

> O Allah, glory and praise are for you, and blessed is your name, and exalted is your majesty; there is no God but you. I seek shelter in Allah from the rejected Satan. In the name of Allah, the most merciful, the most kind.

> Allahu Akbar. Glory to my Lord, the great.

(Three times)

> Allah hears those who praise him. Our Lord praise be to you.

> Allahu Akbar. Glory to my Lord, the highest.

(Three times)

> Allahu Akbar.

He rests a moment, then prostrates himself on the floor again, repeating the words in the last picture.

Salah ends by repeating Allahu Akbar.

> Allahu Akbar.

After Salah is complete, own prayers are said.

▼ Different prayer positions

Think of a peaceful place. This might be known to you, or in your imagination. It is a place to be still, alone, carefree, undisturbed.

We all need peace and privacy at times. It helps to relieve stress and anger that we can bottle up so easily.

Prayer, for a Muslim, is partly about this sense of space and peace. By turning to God five times a day, Muslims unload their worries, ask forgiveness, and seek peace of mind. A Muslim girl once said, 'Saying my prayers and reading the Qur'an really makes me feel at peace. It's good.'

Muslims also remind themselves that they are dependent upon their creator. They did not make themselves and they have no power over the gift of life.

Muslims can say their own prayers anywhere, at any time. True prayer comes from the heart. However, we also express ourselves with our bodies. For example, Christians might kneel, cross themselves or raise their hands in the air, while Muslims bow low, kneel, and cup their hands in prayer.

1 Think about your ideal peaceful place. Describe this and draw it.
2 How often do you try to be alone, and find some space to think and calm down? What sort of things do you do?
3 What value do Muslims find in praying five times a day?
4 What body language is used in Muslim prayer, and what does this express?

◀ *Aliens make sense of earthling places of worship*

Imagine that aliens landed on Earth and watched the different religions at worship. They returned to their planet and described the holy buildings they had seen. These were two of their descriptions:

1 A building with a tower or steeple, with coloured glass in the windows and a cross on top. There were fixed rows of wooden seats inside and a special area at the east end, like a table.
2 A building that had a dome, with a small tower alongside. There was a crescent moon on top. There was an area for washing, and there were no seats at all. An alcove was decorated on one wall.

Which building is Muslim and which is Christian? Give reasons. Try to draw the holy place from the description in 2 above.

The very first mosque was built by Muhammad and his followers in Madinah. Today there are thousands of mosques all over the world. Muslims offer their salah prayers to God in mosques at any time, especially on a Friday lunchtime. The word means 'place of **prostration**' because Muslims bow low to God when praying.

The photograph below shows a typical mosque in Regent's Park, London. The dome helps sound to carry, and this design is also used in Eastern churches.

▲ *The mosque at Regents Park, London*

1 a) Why is there a dome and a tower on a mosque?
  b) Design a new place of worship. What size and shape would it be?

▲ *Note the niche – the mihrab – pointing the way to Makkah, the stand for the sermon to be preached from – the minbar – and the space to make prayer movements*

Inside the small tower, which is called a minaret, is a **muezzin** who sings out the call to prayer. He faces towards the Ka'bah in Makkah when he makes the call in Arabic:

- Allah is the greatest
  Allah is the greatest
  Allah is the greatest
  Allah is the greatest
  I bear witness that there is no God but Allah
  I bear witness that there is no God but Allah
  I bear witness that Muhammad is Allah's messenger
  I bear witness that Muhammad is Allah's messenger
  Rush to prayer, rush to prayer,
  Rush to success, rush to success,
  Allah is the greatest
  Allah is the greatest
  There is no God but Allah

Often today a muezzin uses loudspeakers rather than relying on the strength of his voice.

In a Muslim country, the many mosques in a town will each begin their call to prayer at about the same time and a visitor will hear this echoing all around. It is an impressive and entrancing sound.

Every mosque must have somewhere for Muslims to wash themselves before going to pray. Larger mosques might have an open-air pool or a fountain; smaller ones might only offer cloakrooms. There must be space to leave shoes, too; Muslims always take them off before praying. It stops dust entering the holy building.

Inside, you would find the mosque very bare. There are no seats for the mosque is a place of prayer, or prostration. People pray on their own mats or, in hot countries, they can use the cool floor, though most mosques are carpeted. They stand in rows, shoulder to shoulder. It is a way of showing their brotherhood in their faith.

Muhammad had stopped people praying to idols. He was afraid that people might go back to worshipping them. So there are no paintings or statues in a mosque. Muslims are not allowed to draw animals or people – only God can create them.

33

◀ *Calligraphy and abstract patterns are used to decorate the interior of mosques*

Muslims do not decorate the interior of a mosque with any human or animal designs. They use abstract patterns and calligraphy – decorative forms of Arabic writing.

Mosque walls may be decorated with patterns. Some are **mosaics**; others are drawn in plaster. There may be words as well; sentences taken from the Qur'an.

Often, only men go to the mosque. But, today, women attend services more than in the past. They stand separately from the men so that they don't distract each other. During prayers, Muslims are not allowed to touch someone of the opposite sex. In some Muslim countries, mosques have special areas for women.

This man came across a group of Muslims during his travels.

● As we walked along the hot, dusty road, we heard a strangely beautiful chant fill the air about us. Passing through a group of trees (we saw) on a high wooden tower, a blind Arab, in a white turban. The words which we did not understand fell upon our ears, Allahu Akbar, Allahu Akbar, La llaha illa 'i-Lah (there is no god but God).

Now we noticed that a great number of people were beginning to assemble. They spread long mats upon the ground. The people took off their shoes and sandals and formed long lines, one line falling in behind the other.

We were amazed that no distinctions of any kind were to be found in this **congregation**. Here were white men, yellow men, black men, poor men, wealthy men, beggars, and merchants, all standing side by side with no thought of race or social station in life. Not one single person looked away from the mat in front of him.

---

1 **a)** Write one sentence about each of these: mosque; minaret; minbar; mihrab; Ka'bah.
b) Draw the interior of the prayer hall of a typical mosque and label the mihrab and the minbar.

2 Why do you think that:
a) Muslims wash before praying?
b) Muslims take off their shoes?
c) They don't look at other people?
d) They stand shoulder to shoulder?

3 Read the quotation on this page.
a) What was the blind Arab doing?
b) What were these Muslims about to do?
c) Why do you think they took off their shoes when they were outside?
d) What most impressed the man about this sight?

4 What do you think a Muslim would do if:
a) No water was available?
b) He was in an aeroplane at the time for salah?
c) He was too ill to get to a mosque?

Muslims have religious leaders, called imams. The word 'imam' means 'at the front' – this is the person who leads the prayers. These people are chosen because they have much religious knowledge and because people know them to be good Muslims.

Imams are not usually paid for doing the job. They do the work in their spare time. They earn their money by doing another full-time job. However, in a big mosque, an imam may get paid for being a secretary or caretaker.

▲ *The imam of a mosque in Manchester. Note the prayer mat pointing towards the Ka'bah*

Shaikh Gamal Solaiman is imam at the Regent's Park mosque in London. He describes some of his work.

● An Imam does a lot of things. In addition to sermons, advising people, leading the prayer and so on, he is also busy with other aspects of care. He contacts and visits **bereaved** people, sick people and sometimes people in prison. I start very early and end very late.

The imam's day begins with morning prayer, which can be as early as 3.00 am. Afterwards, he will read the Qur'an. Only then does he have breakfast and perhaps rest before his day's work starts.

His day is spent showing school groups and other visitors round the mosque. There are talks to prepare and letters to answer. People write to him to find out about Islam. In the evening, there are more prayers to lead. Abdul Jalid Sajid is an imam in Brighton. He is also kept very busy:

● I organise many activities: educational and religious programmes at the mosque, financial and building projects, an Islamic school for children each evening and midweek classes for other groups. I visit many schools in the area, and speak to many non-Muslim groups. I am also the Muslim prison and hospital **chaplain** for Sussex.

Many mosques run schools where Muslim children learn about their religion. They are taught to read Arabic so they can learn the Qur'an. Some mosques run these lessons daily. Children go to them after their day's work at school. The Regent's Park mosque is different. The imam explained:

> ● We receive them only one day a week, at weekends. The facilities are limited. I personally think, although three to four hours a week is not enough, coming to the mosque at the end of a very long school day would be a bit much. We are just trying to strike some middle way – neither to overburden the children nor to neglect them.

But Fridays are special. The Arabic word for Friday means *Day of Assembly*. Instead of the usual mid-day prayers, a special act of worship takes place. All adult men must take part. Women are allowed to join in, too. If there is no mosque locally, the prayers can be said anywhere – in a park or on a farm, for instance.

One part of Friday prayer is a khutbah (sermon) given by the imam. It has two parts. In the first part, he will recite from the Qur'an, then explain what it means. In the second part, he will pray for all Muslims everywhere.

But the sermon goes beyond this. The Friday prayer brings all Muslims in a community together. So the imam may use the occasion to talk about any current events which affect Muslims.

Afterwards, the congregation may discuss local problems. Then everyone goes back to work. Friday is not a day of rest for Muslims, as Saturday is for Jews and Sunday is for Christians.

◀ *Children learning about Islam in a madrassah – a religious school at a mosque*

1 Match up the words on the left with the meanings on the right.

imam	Muslims' holy book
khutbah	Muslims' Day of Assembly
Friday	sermon
madrassah	Muslim religious leader
Qur'an	mosque school

2 a) Why do you think a Muslim would agree to become an imam?

b) Which of the following words do you think would describe a good imam? Give reasons for your choices.
unfriendly; helpful; kind; lonely; cheerful; solitary; serious; religious; caring; hopeful.

3 a) Two imams are described in this chapter. Which jobs are done by both of them?

b) Which job do you think an imam would see as most important? Explain how you decided.

4 a) How are the Islamic schools in Brighton and London different?

b) Why does the London mosque hold school only on Saturdays?

c) Do you think it is better for the children to attend every day or not? Give reasons for your view.

5 Suppose a new mosque has opened near where you live but they do not have an imam. Make up an advert or a poster to get someone to do the job. Your answers to **2b)** may give you ideas.

> ● He is a not believer who eats his fill while his neighbour remains hungry by his side.
>
> the Hadith

Muslims believe that everything people have has been given by God. More than that, everything we have *belongs* to God. And that includes our money and possessions.

Strictly speaking, these things are not ours, they are God's. So we should use them as he wishes them to be used. We should spend out money in ways he will approve of. This means giving things to those who need them, not keeping all our money for ourselves.

Muslims believe that poor people have a right to share in the wealth of the rich people. Zakah is a kind of tax which makes sure this happens. It is the third pillar of Islam.

Every Muslim has a duty to pay zakah. Each year, well-off Muslims must give some of their wealth away. It will be used for good causes or to help the poor. Muslims believe it is a sin to let people suffer from hunger or disease. They also think that hanging on to all your wealth is greedy. That, too, is a sin.

The amount to be paid varies. Every Muslim who has money left at the end of the year has to give at least 2.5% (one fortieth) of it away. Farmers must give at least 5% of their crops and a number of animals. Traders give 2.5% of the value of their goods.

Islamic governments take the money from Muslims and share it among the needy. If a Muslim lives in a country which isn't Islamic (such as Britain) then Islamic organisations collect and distribute it.

A Muslim can give zakah direct to another person if he or she wishes. But Muslims believe it is better to give secretly. That way, the giver will not feel proud and the poorer person will not be embarrassed. Muhammad himself said:

> ● The best charity is that which the right hand gives and the left hand does not know of it.

1 The poor and needy

2 People who have recently become Muslims

3 Prisoners-of-war

4 People in debt

5 Muslim tax collectors (for wages)

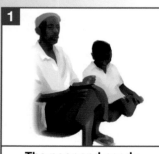

6 Muslims studying Islam

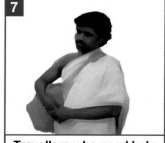

7 Travellers who need help

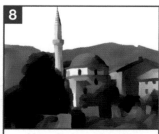

8 Hospitals, schools, libraries and mosques

▲ *The Qur'an sets out who may receive zakah*

Zakah is an act of worship. It is not charity, like giving money on a flag day. It is a duty. It gives to others the wealth that should be theirs.

Nor should people who pay it feel proud. If they were proud of giving the money, they would feel superior to those who receive it. Muslims believe that everyone is equal. Zakah helps to make a fairer society.

A British imam explained how zakah works:

We collect our charity between ourselves. (Then) we seek out any Muslim, for instance a mother whose husband has died and she has several children. Although she gets money from the government, it is still not enough to buy clothes for her children.

But it is left to the conscience of the Muslim. There is nobody coming around asking, 'How much do you earn? How much have you got in the bank?' It is left to your conscience because it is an obligation. If you cheat, which you can do, you're not cheating anybody. You're cheating yourself because you will have to answer on the Day of Reckoning to God why you were so stingy, why you were so mean, why you didn't pay your charity out of the money that God has provided you with.

▲ *A Muslim mother teaches her son to give zakah*

1 Answer these questions in complete sentences:
  a) What is zakah?
  b) Why must Muslims pay zakah?
  c) How is zakah organised in an Islamic country?
  d) How is it done in Britain?

2 **a)** In groups, look at the drawings on page 36. Write down why each of these people might need help:
  (i) a traveller abroad;
  (ii) people who have just become Muslims;
  (iii) prisoners-of-war;
  (iv) Muslims studying Islam.
  b) Which of the groups would you prefer your zakah to go to? Give reasons for your choice.

3 **a)** Why is it a good idea to be told to help the poor?
  b) Can you think of any disadvantages of the idea?

4 **a)** Muslims believe in an equal society. In pairs, discuss whether you think Britain is an equal society. Write down any ways you think it is or is not equal.
  b) Then, write down ways in which you could make a society equal.

5 **a)** If you were to give money to a charity or cause, which would it be? Give reasons for your choice.
  b) How much do you think it would be right to give?

This is the fourth pillar of Islam. It lays down that, at certain times, Muslims must fast – in other words, not eat.

Just like zakah, sawm is an act of worship. Muslims accept they may have to suffer in order to obey God. They know they must accept God's commands at all times. Sawm helps them to remember this.

Fasting helps a Muslim to appreciate how the poor suffer. It is a kind of training which makes it easier for Muslims to be obedient. It also brings Muslims together because they all fast at the same time.

The fasting takes place during the ninth month of the Islamic calendar. The month is called *Ramadan*. One African tribe calls it the 'thirst month'. This was the month when the Qur'an was revealed to Muhammad.

Islamic months are based on the moon and move forward by ten or eleven days each year. The fast lasts for 29 or 30 days (depending on when the new moon is first seen).

All adult Muslims go without food from just before dawn until just after sunset. Even chewing is not allowed. They do not drink, smoke or make love, either. Children under twelve do not have to take part. However, young children are encouraged to fast for a day or two in the month. Two Muslim boys describe what fasting is like:

- You feel the need of the poor and hungry. You're only fasting for a day. You're going to eat food at sunset. But they feel hungry all the time.

  There are also medical benefits. More than half of the cases of heart diseases are due to overweight so by fasting you slim yourself. But if you fast just to slim yourself, you're just wasting your time. You fast because you'll get rewarded in life after death.

  In the beginning you feel hungry but then you get used to it. I went to school and I played athletics although I was fasting. I didn't feel anything because I got used to it.

- You start feeling a bit hungry about four o'clock. But if you start feeling hungry, you read the Qur'an.

▼ *Some adults may not fast during Ramadan and should do so later. Sick Muslims may feed a hungry person for every day they do not fast*

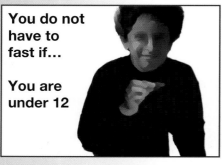

You do not have to fast if…

You are under 12

You are too old

You are pregnant or feeding a baby

You are travelling more than fifty miles

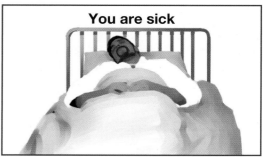

You are sick

◀ This Muslim family shares a good breakfast before the daily fast during Ramadan

Muslims usually have a meal just before dawn during the month of Ramadan. Even so, going without food all day is not easy, no matter what age a person is. It might seem tempting to hide somewhere and have a quick snack. But Muslims know that this cheating may fool other people, but it won't fool God. God can see them all the time.

Muslims are also very careful not to do any bad actions during their fast. No Muslim should tell a lie or break a promise during the whole month.

Each night during Ramadan, Muslims say special prayers. If they can do this in a mosque, they should do so. These prayers involve speaking and listening to as much of the Qur'an as possible. Ideally, Muslims should finish the whole book during Ramadan.

One night is specially important during the month. This is Laylat ul Qadr (the Night of Power). The Qur'an was revealed to Muhammad on this night. By tradition, it is celebrated on an odd-numbered day during the last ten nights of Ramadan. On this night, Muslims should try to stay awake and offer special prayers when God sends down his commandments.

The Qur'an describes that night for Muhammad:

> ● Better is the Night of Qadr than a thousand months. On that night, the angels and the Spirit by their Lord's leave come down with His decrees. That night is peace, till the break of day.
>
> (97:3–5)

---

1 Match up the words on the left with the correct meaning on the right.

Ramadan	Muslims' holy book
Sawm	Islamic ninth month
Laylat ul Qadr	fasting
Qur'an	the Night of Power

2 **a)** Why do you think these people do not fast during Ramadan: children; sick people; pregnant mothers?

b) Design a card that can fit into your pocket with three benefits of fasting for a Muslim. These should involve something about discipline, accepting suffering and sympathy for the poor.

c) Why does the boy read the Qur'an when he feels hungry? Why might this help him?

3 Do you think it's easier to fast in summer or winter? Give reasons.

4 **a)** Do we appreciate things more when we go without them?

b) Can we understand people better if we go through a little of what they suffer?

c) Perhaps you could arrange a sponsored fast or silence for charity. Talk about this in groups.

Hajj (pilgrimage)

Each day all Muslims turn during prayer towards the Ka'bah in Makkah. Once in a lifetime, each Muslim is expected to travel to Makkah, as long as he or she can afford to go. This pilgrimage is called the hajj. It is the final pillar of Islam.

The Ka'bah is seen by Muslims as God's house. They believe it was first built by Adam and later rebuilt by the prophet Abraham and his son Ishmael. It is a simple cube-shaped building, covered with black cloth. But Muslims believe it was the first place ever built just for the worship of God.

Each year, during the twelfth Islamic month, two million Muslims from all over the world go to Makkah. Non-Muslims are not allowed into the city.

The hajj reminds Muslims that they are all equal in the eyes of God. So, as they near Makkah, the pilgrims change their clothes. Instead of ordinary clothes, a male Muslim wears two sheets of unsewn white cloth. Women may wear their everyday clothes, but must be covered from head to ankles.

The white sheets are **symbolic**. They remind Muslims that they must be willing to give up everything for God. It is also a reminder that dead people are wrapped in similar sheets. After death, all fine clothes and wealth are of no value.

The hajj lasts five days. In that time, each Muslim is expected to think of God constantly. On the first day, the pilgrimage begins at Makkah. Each Muslim walks seven times around the Ka'bah, starting at the black stone. Some pilgrims try to kiss it, as a sign of respect.

▲ *Pilgrims on hajj, wearing sheets of white cloth*

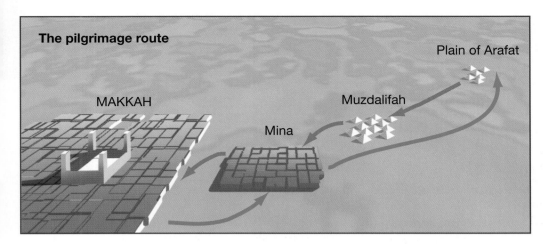

The pilgrimage route

Plain of Arafat

MAKKAH

Muzdalifah

Mina

◀ *The pilgrimage route in Makkah*

Next, the pilgrim goes to two small hills nearby. Here, God ordered Abraham to leave his wife Hagar and son Ishmael. When their water supply ran out, Hagar ran up and down the hills. She was desperately looking for water. Today's pilgrims walk briskly backwards and forwards in memory of her search.

The pilgrims spend the night at Mina. At sunrise on the following day, they go to the valley of Arafat. Thousands of tents are put up specially to protect the pilgrims from the heat. Here, they spend the day meditating in the sun. After sunset, they all leave to spend the night at Muzdalifah. Part of the evening is spent hunting for forty-nine small stones for the next part of the hajj.

Returning to Mina, they set off for three stone pillars. These mark the places where the devil tried to get Ishmael to disobey Abraham. Muslims believe that Ishmael drove the devil away by throwing stones at him. So modern Muslims throw their stones at these pillars. It is a way of showing that they reject evil and wish to follow God.

The pilgrimage ends with a festival. Animals are **sacrificed**. Abraham had been willing to sacrifice his son on God's command. When God spared Ishmael, Abraham sacrificed a ram instead. So modern pilgrims sacrifice a sheep, goat, cow or camel. This is a symbol of how willing they are to give up their lives and possessions for God. Pilgrims eat some of the meat; much of it is given to the poor. Afterwards, they circle the Ka'bah once more; many go on afterwards to Madinah.

All Muslims are expected to go on the hajj at least once in their lifetime if they can afford to do so. However, if they are too sick, they may get someone else to go on their behalf. Many Muslims actually go more than once. It is a great occasion in their lives.

▲ *The decorations on this house in Egypt show that the owner has been on the hajj. Such a man is called a hajji; a woman is called a hajja*

One hajji explained what the pilgrimage was like.

● You find yourself moved and touched. You have become a very small part of a great assembly. Sometimes, you don't worry about the details of the order of events. In fact, the Prophet himself was doing his favourite pilgrimage and certain people came up to him and said, 'I did this before that.' Sometimes, they would say, 'I threw the stone before I shaved' or 'I ordered my sacrifice before I did it.'

All the time, he'd say, 'Do the rest and there is no blame attached.' It is good to know what steps to do but, as far as feeling them, that can only be obtained by going there. It is an amazing experience.

▲ Malcolm X

The ceremonies of hajj revolve around:
- respect (circling the Ka'bah)
- remembering God's care (wandering along Hagar's route)
- turning from evil (throwing stones at the stone pillars)
- offering something to God (sacrificing an animal).

The prophet Abraham is associated with many of these things, and the Ka'bah is said to have been the place where he was going to offer his son, Ishmael, in sacrifice.

Muslims on hajj are reminded that they are all equal: no matter what race they are, or how rich they might be, they are all children of God. This was brought home to one black Muslim leader from the USA, Malcolm X.

Malcolm had joined a black Muslim movement to protest at the poor conditions that black Americans were kept in, and the widespread **prejudice** that was in US society.

This was in the 1960s. He saw the white man as the enemy, the very devil, but when he made his first hajj, he was shaken. Here were people of all races, side by side, helping each other and worshipping. He sat in between two white men on one occasion, and had to receive a sip of water from one, and share the cup with the other. This changed Malcolm's views, and he returned determined to try to co-operate with anyone who would help – white or black.

1 a) Write down one thing which each of these people did in or around Makkah:

(i) Abraham;   (ii) Hagar;   (iii) Ishmael.

b) For each event, write down what modern Muslims do to remember them.

2 a) Put these events from the hajj in the order in which they happen:

(i)   stoning the pillars at Mina

(ii) putting on ihram (pilgrims' clothes)

(iii) sacrificing an animal

(iv) spending the day at Arafat

(v)   walking between the two hills

(vi) going seven times round the Ka'bah

b) Write down one event which is missing from your list.

3 In groups, talk about times:

a) when you have wanted to show respect and praise to someone;

b) when you have needed help and someone has come to your aid;

c) when you have felt sorry for something you have done, and you've made a **resolution** not to do it again;

d) when you have gone out of your way to help someone.

e) Make a group presentation based upon these things, on a piece of A3 paper.

4 What spiritual benefits does going on hajj have for a Muslim? Read the quotation from the hajji and the story about Malcolm X again.

● Birth

If a child has Muslim parents, he or she is considered to be a Muslim at birth. But children are a gift from God. So the parents are honoured that he should give them a new life.

The first words a Muslim baby hears are the call to prayer in Arabic (printed on page 32). This is called the Adhan and is spoken into the baby's right ear. Sometimes a shorter version of the Adhan (Iqamah) is then whispered in his or her left ear.

Back from hospital, a small piece of softened date or honey is gently rubbed around the baby's gums. Muslims pray that the child may have a sweet, trouble-free life. However, the main ceremony comes seven days after the birth. This is called aqiqah.

First, the child's head is shaved of all its hair. In theory, gold or silver equal to the weight of this hair is then given to the poor. But it depends how well-off the family is. Sometimes, much more is given. Today, current money (like £5 notes) can be given instead.

Next, the baby is given a name. This may include one of the ninety-nine names of God such as Abdul Khaliq 'Servant of the Creator'. If not, it could be a prophet's name or the name of someone in Muhammad's family.

Afterwards, friends and neighbours come for a meal. Usually, a lamb or a goat will have been killed. Whatever it is, some of the food will be given to the poor. This is what happens at one British mosque.

> ● The father will bring the food and will invite everybody in the mosque to join. Usually, everybody present in the mosque will go and attend. Naturally, there will be many people. Poverty is relative. There may not be many people here as poor as in Bangladesh.

Muslim boys are circumcised soon after birth.

As soon as possible, the child will begin learning Arabic letters so that he or she can read the Qur'an. At first, the child listens to an adult reading the Qur'an, then repeats it word by word. As soon as possible, he or she will be learning parts of the book by heart.

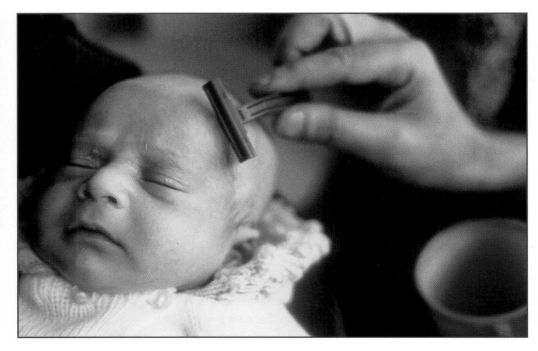

◀ *The aqiqah ceremony where a baby's head is shaved of all its hair*

● Death

▶ Muslim funeral customs vary from one country to another. These villagers in Pakistan are carrying the corpse to the cemetery

Death is always an occasion for sadness. But a dying Muslim may feel a kind of happiness. All Muslims believe in a life after death. And, on the Day of Judgment, loved ones will meet again.

A Muslim who knows he or she is about to die will repeat: 'There is no God but Allah, and Muhammad is his messenger.' After death, the body will be washed and wrapped in white cloths – three for a man, five for a woman. If the dead person has made the hajj to Makkah, the body will be wrapped in the white pilgrim's clothes.

> ● If the law requires people to be buried in a coffin, the religious teaching is to respect such a law. I think how a person is buried is a matter of custom, rather than religious law. What is necessary is to maintain the dignity of death. The body should not be cremated, broken or left exposed.

The burial takes place as soon as possible. Cremation is forbidden. Muslims try to bury their dead so that the head is facing towards the Ka'bah. As the earth is put over the body, people recite from the Qur'an: 'We created you from it and deposit you into it and from it will take you out once more.'

Seven days after the burial, relatives often go back to the grave. It is a mark of respect. Of course, the relatives are sad but they remember the words of Muhammad. He taught that a good Muslim will have left behind three great gifts for others. The first of these is the helpful possessions he has left behind; the second is knowledge; the third is the example which he has given his children. They, too, will grow as Muslims and praise God. For that, they will always have the dead person to thank.

---

1 a) Islam teaches Muslims to care for the poor. What actions in this chapter help the poor?

b) Muslims are not allowed to have expensive gravestones. Why do you think that is?

c) Do you think it would be better if no one had gravestones? Explain your answer.

2 a) What three gifts may a dead Muslim leave behind?

b) Who could benefit from each of these? (Give three different answers.)

c) Which do you think is the most important of these gifts? Give a reason for your choice.

d) Think of someone you respect. Do you think that person would be pleased with how you live your life? Explain your answer.

- O mankind, be mindful of your duty to your Lord who created you from a single soul and from it created its mate and from the two created many men and women.

  Qur'an 4:1

Marriage is very important to Muslims. Most of the prophets, including Muhammad, were married. Muslims believe that the Qur'an encourages them that they should get married.

This applies to both men and women. Islam gives equal rights to men and women. In fact, a Muslim wife keeps her own name after marriage; also, any property she owned before the marriage remains hers. And her husband must provide her with whatever help she was used to having before marriage. Muhammad, in the Hadith, declares, 'How can you beat your wife like a camel when a moment later you will make love to her?'

What makes Muslim marriages different to most Western marriages is that the parents try to find a suitable bride or groom. Sometimes, the boy and girl do not even meet until after the parents have agreed. This is known as an arranged marriage. Love comes after the couple get married, not before.

MW916: Nineteen-year-old Moroccan computer student, kind natured, seeks equally pious Muslim for future life together.

MW911: Scottish Muslim, age eighteen, training as psychiatric nurse, 5ft. 7in., likes writing, seeks suitable lifelong partner.

▲ *Advertisements like these are placed in newspapers and magazines by Muslim parents*

This does not mean the couple has no say in the matter. Both partners must agree before the marriage goes ahead. However, most youngsters seem to trust their parents to make these choices for them. Muslims believe that married people know best what is needed for a good marriage.

45

◄ *Muslim marriage ceremonies vary around the world. They are organised according to each country's laws and customs. This wedding is taking place in Pakistan*

► *This Muslim bride is signing her marriage contract*

This Muslim woman describes how her marriage was arranged:

> ● I was just about to go to Birmingham to start my law degree but my mother felt that for a girl of nineteen to go away from home for the first time . . . was unacceptable. She felt that I had to be married. She felt that marriage would provide a kind of barrier round me, saying, 'Keep off. Married.'
>
> So I was married. It was an arranged marriage, as is (normal) in many Asian families. I knew my husband beforehand. I knew his **temperament** and we got on pretty well anyway.

The two sets of parents will fix the marriage contract. This includes a dowry. This is money or jewellery given by the man to his future wife. She owns this and can do with it as she pleases. Some may keep it as security in case they split up.

This does not happen often. Muslims are allowed to divorce but it is not encouraged. Rather, the couple are encouraged to sort out their problems first. The Hadith says, 'Of all the lawful things, the one which God dislikes most is divorce.'

Muslim weddings are simple affairs, although everyone wears their very best clothes. The marriage can take place at a mosque or at the bride's home. Two witnesses must be present. There may be a reading from the Qur'an and sweets are shared out. The next day, the bridegroom gives a feast for all their relatives and friends.

Muslim men are allowed to marry more than one wife. They may have up to four. But this is rare. Muhammad said that a man must treat each wife equally and very few Muslims can afford to do this. It may happen if the first wife is unable to have children. However, it is not done in countries such as Tunisia and Britain, where it is against the law.

1 Answer these questions in complete sentences:
   a) What is an arranged marriage?
   b) What is a dowry and who pays it?
   c) Why is it rare for a Muslim to have more than one wife?
   d) Where do Muslim marriages take place?
   e) What is Muslims' attitude to divorce?

2 a) How do you think Muslim parents would go about choosing a bride or groom?
   b) List
   (i) the advantages and (ii) the disadvantages of letting your parents make the choice.

3 a) Who will choose the person you marry?
   b) How will that person make this choice? Answer in detail.
   c) Does this mean the marriage will be a success? Give reasons.
   d) Do you think that arranged marriages are more successful than non-arranged marriages? Explain your answer carefully.

4 As a class, compare your answers to **2b).** Which is the longer list?

Muslims believe that family life is essential for a healthy society. So the Qur'an lays down very clear guidelines for family life. No child, it says, should cause harm to his or her parents. They should be loved and cared for. This conversation took place between a man and Muhammad.

> ● Man: Who deserves the best care from me?
> Muhammad: Your mother.
> Man: Who else after that?
> Muhammad: Your mother.
> Man: Who else?
> Muhammad: Your mother.
> Man: Then who else?
> Muhammad: Your father.

As they grow older, parents may need to be supported by their children. This may mean having the parents living with them or helping them out with money. This duty continues until the parents' deaths.

Above all, parents may expect their children to obey them. So family ties in Muslim families are often stronger than those in non-Muslim families. Obedience is a duty, partly in return for what the parents have done for the children in the past.

> ● Your Lord has ordered that you worship none but Him and [show] kindness to your parents. Whether either of them or both of them attain old age in your life, never to say to them, 'Ough' nor be harsh with them, but speak to them kindly.
>   And serve them with tenderness and humility and say, 'My Lord, have mercy on them, just as they cared for me as a little child.'
>   Qur'an 17:23–24

However, parents are not always right. The Qur'an gives a number of examples of parents making mistakes. So children should also be aware of what God wishes. If there is a conflict, the child should do as God would wish.

Muslim girls and boys are expected to work hard at school and do well. Muslims believe that education makes good human beings. As a result, Muslims tend to be very law-abiding. An imam said this:

> ● The Qur'an requires children to respect their parents and be kind to them. The Prophet says if your parents are angry with you, this may bring you the anger of God as well. So it is always hammered, especially in Western countries, with the sense of freedom here.

▲ *This Muslim family worship together in their home*

◄ *This young girl and her great grandmother live in the same house, part of an extended family*

But parents, too, have duties. Muhammad said that people who are kindest to their families show the most perfect faith. He himself was fond of children; he believed that Muslims would become known for their kindness to children.

> ● Parents have to set an example. That is one of the functions of the **extended family**, when three generations are living together. The grandchild will see how his father is treating his father. Of course, I can't say all children are obedient and respectful to their parents. But I think that Muslims are more fortunate than others.
>
> Shaikh Gamal Solaiman

The Qur'an makes it clear that every child has a right to be treated equally. No parent should ever harm their own child. If the parents are dead, the nearest relatives must care for the **orphan**. If there are no relatives, then other Muslims should take on this task.

Living in an extended family used to be more common in the West, with grandparents and relatives either in the same house or down the street. People used to settle in areas where they were brought up and did not usually move away. With greater access to education, and better transport, this has broken down. People expect to leave the home area and make a new life in another area.

There are pros and cons to living in an extended family. There is more help and support, but there are also more people to please and likes and dislikes to deal with.

1 **a)** Write down two duties which Muslim children owe their parents.
b) Do you think these are good rules to live by? Give reasons.
c) Write down two duties which Muslim parents owe their children.
d) Do you think these are good rules to live by? Give reasons.

2 **a)** How do Muslim children show respect for their parents?
b) How do you show respect for yours? (If you don't, say why.)
c) Think carefully! How can parents show respect for children?

3 **a)** Which of the following do you think your parents would like you to be when you grow up: honest; kind; successful; rich; happy; popular; religious; truthful; trusting; a loving parent; hard-working?
b) Write down the two things you would most like to be. Explain how you chose them.

4 **a)** What are the advantages and disadvantages of living in an extended family?
b) Why don't many non-Muslims live in extended families in Britain today?

▲ *These Muslim schoolgirls wear clothes to cover their bodies completely*

Muslim parents tend to be strict with their children. They are not encouraged to go to parties; mixed dancing is not allowed. Muslim parents will not approve of boyfriends and girlfriends. Sex outside marriage is forbidden.

These rules can cause problems for Muslims living in a non-Muslim country, such as Britain. Muslim teenagers see other teenagers going to nightclubs and wearing Western clothes. They might want to copy this. This can start arguments between parents and children.

Many Muslim children would not be allowed to do the things opposite. This is to protect them from trouble and the temptation of sex before marriage. Traditional dress for a Muslim woman covers her body. This is also to keep Muslim culture and traditions alive in a country where they are in the minority.

Attitudes vary, though, and some Muslim parents become more Westernised and accept current fashions.

1. Write a role play between a Muslim girl and her mother. She wants to go out with her friends and wear Western clothes.

2. Write a role play about a Muslim boy who is out with some non-Muslim friends and they start drinking.

▲ *Western customs frowned upon by Muslims*

Many Western people think that Muslim women do not get equal treatment with men. In fact, the aim of Islam is quite the opposite.

At the time of Muhammad, pagan Arabs saw women as possessions to be bought and sold. Islam, on the other hand, gave women an important place. They were to be honoured and respected. 'Paradise,' said Muhammad, 'lies at the feet of your mothers.'

Muslim women's rights are equal to those of men. Muslims believe that God created all people equal – but not **identical**. Men and women, they argue, have different qualities.

Their duties are different. Muslim men's duties are work and public affairs. A Muslim woman's main duties are to look after the home and care for her family. This does not mean that a Muslim woman may not work outside her home. Many Muslim women are nurses, teachers or doctors. In farming villages, Muslim men and women share the work.

▲ *This Muslim woman keeps her face covered in public*

> ● During the time of the Prophet, the women worked, the women [took part] in wars. According to the Qur'an, I can see no problem. The women are allowed to work and they should **participate** in life. They have equal legal rights and equal obligations. This is what Islam gives the woman in theory. In practice, you find it quite different.
>
> Egyptian woman

In fact, a Muslim woman's freedom mainly depends on which country she lives in. And this freedom can change, depending on who rules the country.

In Saudi Arabia, for example, women are not allowed to drive cars. Yet many go to university and go on to do important jobs. There is even a women's bank, run by women for women customers only. Even so, most Saudi women lead their lives entirely inside the family circle. Very few women go out to work.

The Qur'an gives advice about clothing. Islam does not force Muslims to wear any particular kind of clothes. But Muslims believe that people are the best of God's creatures. So their dress should always be decent.

There are different rules for men and women. Men should not wear cloth such as silk or clothes decorated with gold. It may make them proud. So fine clothes are to be worn only by women.

Men are expected to cover their body from the navel to their knees. Women are asked to cover their whole body – except for the face, hands and feet. This can cause problems in a non-Muslim country, as an imam explained:

> ● A Muslim girl can go swimming with other girls. The law is relaxed. She can go in a swimming costume with girls and a lady instructor. But swimming with men, there would be a problem.

Women may not wear skin-tight clothes or anything which reveals their figure. The aim is to stop women from tempting men and from being gossiped about. In Iran, women wear long black gowns, except when they are working.

Some Muslims believe that women should also cover part of their face when out of doors. That is why some Muslim women wear veils. Others think that only Muhammad's wives had to do this. They believe modern women can copy this if they wish.

However, once inside her own home, there are no restrictions. Islam does not stop a woman dressing up or wearing make-up for her family; it only tries to stop her attracting the eyes of strangers.

These Muslim women give their views about clothes:

● The Muslim girl has to come to terms with the fact that she's different. My parents encouraged me to wear trousers. Although I looked very odd in the beginning, I told the other girls at school why I had to wear them and that they should respect me as I respected what they were wearing as well.

● I could cover myself fully and what I'm saying would have the same meaning as if I'm not covered. I'm not an object that needs to be admired or looked at. I could just be a voice or a face and any words would still have the same meaning. Muslim women are trying to move towards an image where we don't have to sell our looks to get heard.

● When I was nine, my parents wanted me to wear this scarf. I used to go to school with a scarf and I used to hate it. When I was twelve, I used to feel desperately ashamed. I actually started liking to wear it and feeling proud of wearing it when I was eighteen.

▲ *These Muslim women are wearing the national dress of Pakistan*

1 **a)** On your own, write down the ways in which you think men and women are equal.
   b) Now, write down any ways in which you think they are not equal.
   c) In groups, discuss your answers. You will need one person who will report to the class about the group's answers. So you need to try to reach agreement.
   d) The woman wearing a veil on page 50 believes this helps her to be free. Why do you think this is? What do you think of this?
   e) Do you think Muslim women are really equal to men? Be ready with reasons.
2 You need some daily newspapers for this question.
   a) In groups, go through each paper and try to find examples of unequal treatment of women. Stick your item in your exercise book and explain how it shows that women are not equal.
   b) Now, look for an example of a woman being exploited. Describe the item and write down how the woman is being exploited.
   c) Which of your examples would Muslims disapprove of? Explain how you decided.
3 **a)** In what ways are women taking leading roles in Western society?
   b) What do you think of some Western men staying at home to raise the children?

Human beings need to celebrate special events and they throw parties, sharing food and drink. They give gifts and visit their families. We need some fun in life, with things to look forward to, and remembering birthdays, wedding anniversaries or other special dates helps us to value those things.

Religions have festivals, too, which come around each year. Special stories or events are remembered in their faith. Muslim festivals are called *Id*. There are two main festivals: Id-ul-Fitr and Id-ul-Adha.

▲ *These boys in Egypt are celebrating a birthday*

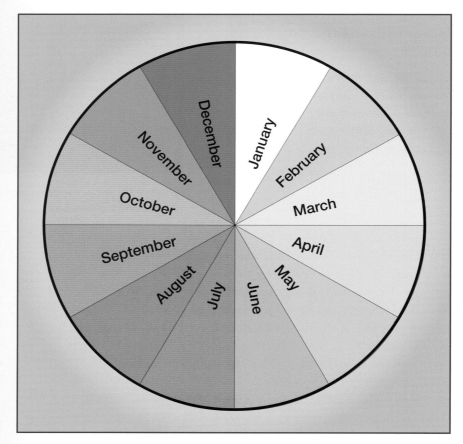

▲ *What celebrations do we have each year?*

1 Copy the pie chart into your books over a page. On each month, write in any special events that are celebrated in your family. You might need to explain some more unusual ones below. Holidays could be included if you tend to go at the same time each year, or if you regularly go to the same place.

◄ *These goats have been specially fattened and decorated to be sacrificed at Id-ul-Adha*

Id times are events of great joy for Muslims all over the world. But they are not held purely for fun and enjoyment. They are duties, to give thanks to God.

Id-ul-Fitr

Id-ul-Fitr was begun by Muhammad himself and comes after the end of Ramadan, on the first day of the next month. Muslims thank God for the Qur'an and for helping them to fast throughout the month. (If necessary, they will ask his forgiveness for any failures.)

In Muslim countries, Id-ul-Fitr is a national holiday. Muslims visit friends and relations, wearing their best clothes. The well-off give to the poor so that they, too, may enjoy the day. Everyone eats special food and children are given presents. This Muslim boy gave his view of Id-ul-Fitr.

> ● We do what is prescribed for us. We take it as it comes, as part of life. As kids, in Ramadan, you come to the mosque and get a chance to meet your friends. At Id, everybody gives each other presents. That's probably the favourite festival.

Above all, Id is a time for prayer. The festival begins with prayers at the mosque. Unlike festivals in other religions, Muslims do not dance or go to nightclubs; they do not go to parties. It is more a time for the family to get together; a chance to meet your neighbours.

Id-ul-Adha

The second major festival, Id-ul-Adha, was also begun by Muhammad. It means festival of sacrifice. This festival remembers the time when Abraham was ready to sacrifice Ishmael because God commanded it. By taking part, modern Muslims are showing that they, too, are ready to sacrifice their lives for God.

Id-ul-Adha comes towards the end of the hajj. It also begins with prayers at the mosque. This day, too, is a public holiday in Muslim countries. Even in non-Muslim countries, many Muslims take a day off to celebrate.

They sacrifice an animal, just as God eventually told Abraham to sacrifice a sheep. So the event is symbolic. God does not want the animal (or its meat); God wants Muslims to show him their **devotion**. The meat itself is shared with friends and relatives and, of course, the poor.

▲ *These Kenyan boys are dancing to celebrate Muhammad's birthday on 12th Rabi ul-Awwal*

▲ *Muslims send cards like this to celebrate Id-ul-Fitr*

A British Muslim describes Id-ul-Adha:

> ● My feelings were feelings of joy. It was a day to celebrate a great occasion that had taken place hundreds of years ago in the Mounts of Arafat. It was a day when I could ask for forgiveness. It was a day when I could join hundreds of other people who were worshipping their creator. It was a day when I am convinced that my prayers are answered.

Apart from these two major festivals, Muslims also celebrate four events in Muhammad's life. Strictly speaking, they are not festivals but most Muslims remember them.

Laylat-ul-Qadr has already been mentioned. This remembers the night when Muhammad was first given the words of the Qur'an. Muslims spend the night in prayer, reading from the Qur'an.

Ashura, on the 10th Muharram, reminds Muslims of the day when Noah left his ark and Moses saved the Israelites from the Egyptians. Muslims fast for two days. Another festival is mentioned in the caption above.

1 Match up the events on the left with what they celebrate on the right:

Id-ul-Fitr	Muhammad's birthday
Id-ul-Adha	Noah leaving the ark
Laylat-ul-Qadr	Festival of Sacrifice
Ashura	the end of fasting
12th Rabi ul-Awwal	the night of power

2 Why do you think:

a) Muslims wear their best clothes for Id-ul-Fitr?

b) They do not go to parties or nightclubs on this occasion?

c) Muslims remember Muhammad's birthday?

d) The Id card has no people drawn on it?

e) The Muslim is sure his prayers are answered at Id-ul-Adha?

3 Look at the Id card shown above. Notice the vivid colours. Design your own Id card to send to a Muslim friend. Remember that there will be no pictures of people on it. If you draw it on a piece of card, you could copy the Arabic writing on to the back of it.

> Say Allah's name (Bismillah) and eat with your right hand and eat from near you.

An essential part of everyday life is food. We have already seen that Muslims fast during Ramadan. So it is not surprising that Islam has rules about eating, too.

After all, food affects our health. And Islam tries to create a healthy society. So Muslims can eat and drink anything which is pure and good – but not too much of it.

The things they can eat and drink are called *halal*. These are the lawful things. There is, however, a list of banned foods and drinks. These are known as *haram*.

▲ *British Muslims can shop at a store such as this one*

Muslims are allowed only to eat meat which has been killed in the name of God. That is why many Muslims buy meat only from Muslim butchers. The butcher will have said 'God is great' three times over the animal before killing it. If there is no Muslim butcher locally, many Muslims would buy from a Jewish butcher. Their meat is also prepared in a special way.

An animal slaughtered by halal methods is thought to be killed more humanely. Not only is its life offered up to God in thanksgiving, but it is approached from behind so as not to startle it, after it has been separated from other animals (so as not to cause them distress). The knife is extra sharp so that the cut is swift and death comes quickly. This also lets the blood flow out, as Muslims are not allowed to eat the blood of an animal. This is very different from Western abattoirs, where animals are herded in together and are pushed and shoved like feelingless objects.

Fish and vegetables are allowed but no Muslim may eat an animal which has been strangled to death. No pig meat is allowed. Even lard is haram. So are all animals or birds which are already dead. Finally, Muslims do not eat animals which themselves eat meat.

- They're considered to be bad for the body. Anything that is bad for the body is also bad for the spirit as well.

No committed Muslim drinks alcohol or takes drugs. Muslims believe that wines and beer lead to all kinds of social problems. Islam wants to create a healthy society. Alcohol can lead to drunkenness – and that can create trouble. No alcohol at all is allowed in Saudi Arabia.

> ● O you who believe, wine and gambling . . . are filthy tricks of Satan; avoid them so that you may prosper. Satan wants to **incite** . . . hatred among you by means of wine and gambling and prevent you from remembering Allah and from Salat. So will you not give them up?
>
> Qur'an 5:90–91

Muslims say thanks to God, and wash, before and after each meal. The eldest member of the family eats first, unless there is a guest. No one leaves the table until the last person has finished.

Some schools with many Muslim children have introduced halal food at lunchtime. Following the food laws in a non-Muslim country can be difficult – what about biscuits that might contain certain animal fats, for example? The Muslim faith says that a believer should try to follow the food laws where possible, but they can be relaxed when it is too difficult. Personal survival must come first.

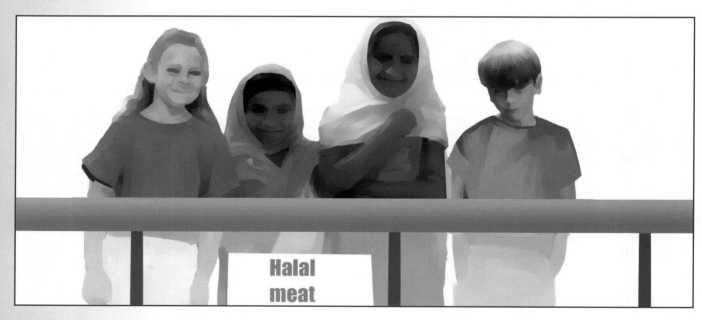

▲ *Halal food is served in some British schools*

1 What is the difference between halal and haram?

2 **a)** What rules must be followed to slaughter an animal by the halal method?

b) Why do Muslims argue that this is more humane than in Western abattoirs?

3 **a)** How can you tell that the shop in the photograph is run by Muslims?

b) Why is it difficult for Muslims to eat in English cafés and restaurants?

4 Read why Muslims are not allowed to drink alcohol. Then design a poster reminding them of their duty. It must be eye-catching, with a good slogan.

5 **a)** Are there any reasons why you would not eat certain foods?

b) What might a vegetarian do if the only food offered in a restaurant included meat?

There are many Muslim countries in the world today. They all follow Islam. If they acted together, they would be a powerful force in the world. Yet, on some matters, they disagree. Indeed, one dispute within Islam goes back to its very earliest days.

After Muhammad's death, caliphs were chosen to lead the Muslim people. The fourth caliph was Ali, Muhammad's son-in-law, but he was killed in a struggle for power.

One group of Muslims believe that, after Ali's death, his sons should have taken over as caliphs. They believe that Ali's **descendants** are the true leaders of Islam. This group is called Shi'ah; its members are Shi'ites. The word Shi'ah means *group*. They did not accept the later caliphs and chose their own imams instead.

The main Muslim group is the Sunni Muslims. The word 'sunni' means '**orthodox**'. They agree with the Shi'ites on most religious matters, but they supported the caliphs who were chosen after Ali.

Because there have always been fewer Shi'ites, they have never enjoyed the same power as the Sunni Muslims. Major Arab nations, such as Saudi Arabia, are still ruled by Sunni Muslims today. In the past, Sunni Muslims in the Lebanon shared power with the Christians. The Shi'ites were poor; they had little influence.

▼ *A Shi'ite shrine in Syria*

All this changed in recent years. Iran is the main home of the Shi'ah Muslims, and a revolution there in 1979 restored many Islamic laws and customs. Other Shi'ite groups have taken courage from this and have campaigned for their rights.

After the revolution, Iran was taken over by its religious leaders, called ayatollahs. The word means 'sign of God'.

The leading ayatollah was Ayatollah Khomeini. He made Iran an Islamic state once more. Islamic laws, based on the Qur'an, were introduced. Alcohol was banned. Women could only appear in public with their heads and bodies fully covered.

A true Islamic state is run in the same way that the Prophet Muhammad organised the Muslim community in Madinah. In an Islamic state, the head of state (or a deputy) is supposed to lead the daily prayers at a central mosque. This was how Muhammad led his state. Many Muslims would like to see the practice brought back.

▲ *During the Ashura celebrations, which mark the death of the Shi'ite Al-Hussein, some men and boys deliberately injure themselves. Shi'ite Muslims have special respect for those who are prepared to suffer or die for their faith*

▲ *Ayatollah Khomeini*

1 Answer these questions in complete sentences:

a) What are the two main Muslim groups called?

b) Which group is the larger?

c) About what did Shi'ah and Sunni Muslims disagree?

d) Name one Sunni country and one Shi'ite country.

e) Why do you think that some men and boys injure themselves at the Ashura celebrations?

f) In which country was there an Islamic revolution in 1979?

g) What were the results of this?

2 a) In groups, work out what you would expect life to be like in an Islamic state. You may need to read earlier chapters again to remind yourself of some ideas.

b) How would it be different from life in Britain today?

c) Now, compare your answers to **a)** and **b)**. What do you think a Muslim would miss most by living in Britain?

No one knows exactly how many Muslims there are in the world today. But we do know that Islam is the second largest religion after Christianity and it is the world's fastest-growing religion.

Yet, for most of the last 200 years, it was very different. In the eighteenth and nineteenth centuries most Muslim countries were under Western control. By contrast with Europe, Muslim countries were poor.

Since the Second World War, most Muslim countries have become independent once more. Many have become richer by selling oil. So Muslims have once again become a powerful force in world affairs. Islam is once again spreading. Muslims believe this is a gift from God.

Other world powers discovered the power of Islam in 1973 when Israel was at war with Egypt and Syria, both of which are Arab countries. The Arabs were supported by most other Muslim countries. They objected to Israel having land which had once been Arab. They also objected to the United States supporting Israel.

So they used a new weapon to support Egypt and Syria. They stopped selling oil to the United States. The result was a world oil shortage. Almost overnight, prices trebled.

When the ban ended, the Arabs made it clear that they would use oil as a political weapon again, if they chose. After two centuries of being controlled by the West, the Muslims felt that at last they would be taken seriously.

The revival of Islam is seen most clearly in Iran, which did not join in the 1973 **boycott**. After the 1979 revolution, a large number of the people voted to set up an Islamic state. This means that their laws are based on the Qur'an.

Many Iranians were pleased with the changes. Politics is part of their religion. They believe that, if the state follows religious laws, its political problems will be solved. But not all Muslim countries approved. In 1980, Iraq and Iran began a war which went on until 1988.

What made the Iranian revolution special was that its leaders wanted Shi'ite groups elsewhere to fight for power, too. So Iran supported Shi'ite groups in other countries, such as the Lebanon.

▲ *Iranian soldiers at prayer during the war with Iraq*

Iran would like to see all Muslims living under strict Islamic rule.

The Iranian revolution worried many non-Muslim countries. In the former Soviet Union, the Muslim population is growing fast. One in five of the world's Muslims lives there. Its leaders have been worried that Soviet Muslims might demand the right to rule themselves by Islamic law.

The revolution put Islam back into the spotlight. Muslims believe that when all Muslims around the world come together, the world will be a more peaceful place.

The traditional Muslim law is called 'the Shari'ah', 'the Way'. This applies Islam to all aspects of society. It is largely based upon the Qur'an, plus later, oral traditions. It means women have to adopt traditional dress, and physical punishments such as the death penalty, or **severing** a thief's hand, are carried out.

Some Muslims want to return to the Shari'ah, rejecting Western values with all the cheating, drug addiction and sexual loose living. Others do not, and want more personal freedom guaranteed by the State. Also, there are disputes on how to follow the Shari'ah today. Some rules were wise in the seventh century, but times have changed. Others argue that some traditions, such as stopping women working outside the home, are not actually a part of the original Shari'ah and are against the Qur'an.

Muslims have divisions and arguments like any other faith. Many Muslims feel that there should be more tolerance of other factions and they reject the type of Islam set up by the Iranian revolution.

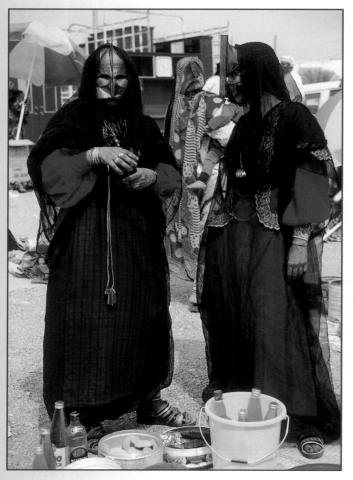

◄ *Veiled Muslim women selling roadside drinks. Some Muslim countries would not allow them to do this*

1 a) If everybody were the same religion, would the world be at peace? Explain your answer.

   b) Why do you think people of the same religion still have disagreements?

2 a) Why do you think some Westerners are choosing to become Muslims?

   b) From what you have read, suggest three major changes this would mean in their lives.

3 Iran and Iraq are both Muslim countries, yet they went to war. Does this mean:

   a) their leaders are not good Muslims or

   b) Islam does not believe in peace?

   Explain both your answers.

4 Design a suitable flag for Iran after it became an Islamic state. When you have finished, you could compare your efforts with the real thing.

5 a) How much power do religious leaders have in this country?

   b) Do you think religions should have power to force people to behave in a certain way?

◄ *Some scientific instruments developed by Muslims*

The Qur'an encourages Muslims to seek for knowledge. So early Muslim rulers did the same. As a result, Muslims made great contributions to science and mathematics.

Much of their knowledge was needed for religious reasons. They needed to know the hours of prayer. Payment of zakah meant they had to do mathematics.

Arabs brought Arabic numerals (such as 1 and 2) to Europe; Arabs were the first to use zero. More than that, Muslim scholars were the first to work out a full system of decimal calculation. Europeans later took up the idea. Muslims also invented algebra.

Muslim scientists showed special interest in **astronomy** and the stars. They needed to be able to work out the direction of Makkah so that they could prayer wherever they were.

As a result, they discovered many 'new' stars. Europeans still call some today by their Arabic names. They also invented the astrolabe which measures the height of the stars. Western explorers found this useful on their voyages of discovery.

Muslim scientists learned by experiments. In the middle ages, the Christian Church discouraged Western scientists from carrying out experiments. So Muslim scientists took the lead in geography and botany.

▲ *Just some of the Arabic words we still use today*

In medicine, Muslim doctors were more skilled than Christian ones. They relied less on surgery and more on natural drugs and herbs. They stressed good diet and a healthy life. Today, many non-Muslims still turn to Muslim healers for natural treatment of illnesses.

Muslim traders travelled far overseas long before Western explorers such as Columbus. Their maps were some of the finest of their time. Their earliest world maps show the Earth as round. Most Europeans of the time still thought it was flat.

Many books written by ancient Greeks and Romans survive only because they were copied and translated by Muslims. Muslim **scholars** travelled throughout Europe, tracking down ancient **manuscripts**. In turn, people from all over Europe travelled to Muslim universities. Muslims were ahead of Europeans in almost every branch of knowledge.

Muslims have had a tradition of making carpets for well over a thousand years. Muslim tents had little furniture. They had cushions and rugs instead.

Many Muslims today have their own beautiful prayer mats. Often, the weavers of these mats base the whole decoration around a single word, woven over and over again. It is always possible to spot one which has been woven by a Muslim. This carpet expert explains:

> ● In any true Persian or Turkish rug, it should be possible to discover the Deliberate Mistake. Many of the Muslim faith believe that only Allah makes things perfectly; therefore, to weave a perfectly designed rug would be to risk offending him.
>
> I once knew a repairer of rugs who held his belief so firmly that he was in constant trouble with his employer. Just before finishing work on each rug, he would make a deliberate mistake. He explained that, although he was afraid of offending his employer, he was even more fearful of offending Allah.
>
> Caroline Bosley: *Rugs to Riches*

62

1 Copy out and fill in the grid below, using the clues.
  a) Muslims practically invented this.
  b) This Arabic word is still used to mean nought.
  c) Muslim doctors stressed this.
  d) Muslim scholars worked out a system of _____ calculation.
  e) The study of the stars.
  f) Muslim scientists took the lead in this.

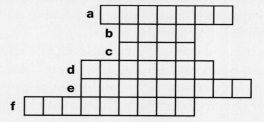

2 You will need a sheet of squared paper. Design a mat, based on either Arabic writing or the design you can see on the mat on page 6. An arch should be included to point in the direction of prayer. It should be suitable for using as a prayer mat.

▲ *Muslims have been making prayer mats and carpets for over a thousand years*

Glossary

assembly – meeting
astronomy – study of the sun, moon, stars, etc
atom – tiny bit

Bedouin – Arab who lives in the desert and has no fixed home
bereaved – deprived (of relations)
boycott – refuse to buy or sell

chaplain – priest in duty at an institution, such as a hospital or prison
civil war – war between people of the same country
clot – mass which is partly solid
compassionate – pitying
compulsion – use of force
compulsory – compelled; required
congregation – meeting of people for worship

descendant – person born into a family, eg child or grandchild
devotion – deep love

empire – group of countries ruled by another country
extended family – family which has more than just parents and their children living together
extremist – holding extreme views, thinking that they are right and everyone else is wrong

foster mother – woman who brings up another woman's child

humility – not being proud

identical – exactly the same
idol – thing that is worshipped, such as a statue
imam – person who leads the prayers in a mosque
incite – urge; encourage

Ka'bah – cube-like building in Makkah towards which Muslims pray

legend – ancient story which many people believed

manuscript – book written by hand
meditating – thinking deeply

minority – a small group of people
mosaic – small pieces of stone which make a pattern
mosque – Muslim building for prayer and worship

niche – hollow in a wall

obituary – writing about a person's life after they have died
obscure – hidden, not obvious or easy to understand
opposed – challenged
orphan – child whose parents are dead
orthodox – views accepted by most people

pagan – person who worshipped many gods
participate – take part in
pilgrim – person on a religious journey to a holy place
prejudiced – having opinions without good reasons
prophet – person who speaks out in the name of God
prostration – bowing down low

recite – say aloud from memory
resolution – a promise to yourself

sacred – holy
sacrificed – offered to God
Satan – the Devil
scholar – person who has a great deal of knowledge
sermon – public talk on religion
severing – cutting off
shrine – sacred place
sin – doing something wrong
stereotyped – saying that everyone in a group has the same behaviour and characteristics
sublime – perfect and beautiful
submission – obedience to a greater power
Sura Yasin – a chapter of the Qur'an
symbolic – used as a symbol (sign) of something else

temperament – what a person is like
treaty – a legal agreement between two groups to make peace

vision – something seen

Index